BLACK MESA

BLACK MESA

Survey and Excavation in Northeastern Arizona · 1968

by

George J. Gumerman

PRESCOTT COLLEGE PRESS · 1970

PRESCOTT COLLEGE STUDIES IN ANTHROPOLOGY NO. 2

Foreword

THE PRESCOTT COLLEGE-BLACK MESA ARCHAEOLOGICAL PROJECT had its genesis in the early summer of 1967. Our Archaeological Survey received a telephone call from Mr. E. R. Phelps, then Vice President for Engineering of the Peabody Coal Company in St. Louis, informing us of his company's intention to undertake large scale strip coal mining on Black Mesa in northern Arizona, and inquiring if we could carry out some initial archaeological reconnaissance for them.

The conversation that followed should be illuminating to archaeologists involved in contracting so-called salvage projects. When we indicated that we would be willing to do the work, we also asked for detailed maps of the land areas to be surveyed so that we could prepare a cost estimate for Mr. Phelps' consideration. He replied, "This is the first time I've heard anything sensible from you archaeologists. Usually you say, 'Don't worry about the cost. It's all for science.' And, frankly, I can't run this coal company on that basis." Our continuing relations with the Peabody Coal Company from that initial conversation have always been conducted in terms of such program budgeting with a view to accomplishing thorough work of high professional standards within the important framework of realistic cost estimates.

The coal company plans to strip mine coal on Black Mesa, crush it at a plant site there, and then transport it through a 274 mile slurry pipe line to a power plant in Nevada across the Colorado River from Bullhead City, Arizona.

Our first surveys involved approximately 100 miles of right-of-way of the slurry line (all within the confines of the Navajo and Hopi reservations), about 100 acres of one strip mine area, several miles of truck haulage road right-of-way, and some 100 acres of the proposed preparation plant site.

This work was accomplished mainly by helicopter reconnaissance from an elevation of 40 to 60 feet above ground surface at an average speed of 20 miles per hour. Landings at all sites observed were made without difficulty. Some additional survey, especially in terrain covered with piñon-juniper, was done on foot. The entire survey was completed in two and one-half days. Three sites were recorded along the slurry line (a Navajo *ramada*, an early Pueblo III Kayenta masonry structure, and a Basketmaker III sherd area), six sites in the initial mining area (four Navajo hogans and two early Pueblo III Kayenta pueblos), and three early Pueblo III structures in the area of the proposed plant site. In March, 1968, the coal company enlarged this latter area and a subsequent survey revealed six additional sites of an early Pueblo III Kayenta affiliation.

During the spring months of 1968, the coal company indicated those sites and areas that would be disturbed by construction in 1969 and, through our field estimates of man-days of excavation time, we prepared accurate and detailed cost estimates for the first season of the project.

It was at this time that the Peabody Coal Company agreed enthusiastically to our suggestion that we involve students as well as Navajo laborers in the excavations and thus convert a salvage operation to an undergraduate field school. During the summer of 1968 we were thus able to provide instruction in archaeological field techniques as well as discussions from specialists in the related fields of ethnobotany, ethnozoology, palynology, archeomagnetism, and dendrochronology for ten students from three colleges and universities.

Actual field work began in June and in the ensuing six weeks six sites were excavated under the direct field supervision of George Gumerman. Prescott College provided all necessary excavation, camp, and vehicular equipment, some of which was obtained through a National Science Foundation, matching funds, undergraduate equipment grant which is hereby acknowledged.

In order to provide Gumerman with adequate time for the student assisted analyses as well as the preparation of the manuscript, his teaching load was reduced to one course (Laboratory Techniques in Archaeology) for the fall quarter immediately following the field session. The support of the President of Prescott College, Ronald C. Nairn, in this as well as in the entire Black Mesa Project has been superb, and all of us concerned are deeply grateful for his dynamic concern with teaching through research as he discussed it in a campfire seminar with students at our field camp toward the close of the 1968 season.

With such academic support and the financial and other cooperation of the Peabody Coal Company, students were trained and new archaeological data for the Black Mesa district were obtained. At this writing a second field season has been completed, analysis and writing are in progress, and a second report should be published within a year.

December 7, 1969

ROBERT C. EULER

Acknowledgments

DESPITE THE FACT THAT THIS REPORT lists a single author, numerous people had a hand in all phases of the preparation of this report from the preliminary site survey to the final editing and typing.

I owe a great debt of gratitude to Robert C. Euler, the Director of the Black Mesa Project, without whom there would be no Black Mesa Project at Prescott College. He initiated the project, accomplished the initial survey, offered wise counsel on his visits to the excavations, made helpful suggestions in editing, and while we enjoyed the fruits of field work he handled the administrative chores of the project with barely a murmur of protest.

The following students who toiled on the mesa in 1968 contributed more than a labor pool. Many of the ideas and thoughts expressed in this volume and in future volumes germinated from discussion with them. Sheila McFarlin, University of Kentucky; Kathleen Wasson and Joyce Rehm, University of Arizona; Kirk Gray, Erik Karlstrom, Henry Grosjean, Heather Murray, Robert Page, John Ware, and Carol Weed, all of Prescott College. Mrs. Nancy Hammack served as Assistant Field Director and Mr. Bruce Harrill of the University of Arizona acted as Dig Foreman.

The following Prescott College students worked in the laboratory after the field session and compiled much of the data on the following pages: Kirk Gray, Heather Murray, Robert Page, John Ware, and Carol Weed.

I thank Joseph P. Van Den Acre, the cook, and Charles Smith, the cook's helper, for serving a ravenous mob (often with unexpected guests) under trying logistic and weather conditions.

The following visitors added immeasureably to the success of the field school as a school by discussing their specialties formally or informally with the students: Robert Rowan of Arizona State University on palaeobotany; Peter S. Bennett of KVL Laboratory on palynology; Hugh Cutler of the Missouri Botanical Garden on ethnobotany; Stanley Olson of the University of Florida on ethnozoology; Albert Johnson of the University of Oklahoma on archeomagnetic dating; William Robinson of the University of Arizona on dendrochronology; Thor Karlstrom of the U. S. Geological Survey on surficial geology; and Jeffrey Dean of the University of Arizona and Alan Olson of the University of Denver, on Anasazi archaeology. In addition, we were visited by the University of New Mexico and University of Arizona field schools, when the latter lost to Prescott College in volleyball and failed to pay off a case of beer.

Numerous logistic problems were encountered in the field as might be expected for the first field operations of a three-year-old liberal arts and science institution. In helping smooth these problems and in assisting us in many ways — not the least in furnishing ice for our drinks and salve for our gnat bites — were the various personnel of Peabody Coal Company listed below: John Arnold, William Kennedy, Gary Nicholson, Kelly Nolan, Ed Phelps, Leonard Sawtelle, Joseph Taylor, and Charles Turner. In addition, Peabody Coal Company deserves our greatest appreciation for sponsorship of these excavations. The funds for excavation of Ariz. D:11:15 were provided by Black Mesa Pipeline, Inc. I wish to thank Mr. Michael Hunter of Black Mesa Pipeline, Inc. for his assistance in administrative matters.

The Navajo laborers, James Cody, Paul Chief, and Jack Chief, toiled many hot hours in what to them must have seemed an endless task.

Permits to excavate and survey were kindly granted by the Navajo Tribal Council and the Hopi Tribal Council as well as the U.S. Department of the Interior and the BIA area offices in Window Rock and Phoenix. Mr. Leland Abel of the National Park Service assisted in the numerous administrative tasks.

Jay Dusard processed the photographs and did the frontispiece sketch and Jeffrey King and Joyce Rehm did the drafting. Mrs. Joyce Anderson accomplished the arduous task of assembling the bibliography and proofreading the manuscript. Alice Maxell typed most of the copy. My wife Sheila helped during the excavations and in the laboratory, as well as taking care of our two children and acting as camp nurse and mother.

I owe a great debt of gratitude to Kayenta scholars such as Jeffrey Dean, Robert Euler, Alexander Lindsay, William Robinson, and Watson Smith, who have helped me formulate questions and clarify problems. In addition, Jeffrey Dean and Floyd Sharrock offered helpful criticism of this manuscript. In innumerable conversations with these men and discussions with students, the origins of many of my ideas and concepts have become muddled. If the germ of an idea expressed in the following pages originated with anybody mentioned above, I apologize.

Cover Etching: "The Way: Mountain Which Appears Black"
by Patricia Vivian

Table of Contents

List of Illustrations

List of Tables

CHAPTER ONE

Introduction

DURING THE MONTH OF JUNE and part of July, 1968, the Center for Anthropological Studies operated an archaeological field school on Black Mesa on the Hopi and Navajo Indian reservations under sponsorship of the Peabody Coal Company of St. Louis, Missouri. A total of eight sites was excavated and 56 sites were surveyed. What follows is a descriptive report of these investigations.

It should be emphasized that this report is mainly descriptive, and that interpretations, where they occur, are tentative. These words are being written after the second year of survey and excavation, and it can be assumed that there will be several years more work on northeastern Black Mesa. The decision was made, therefore, to produce descriptive reports of each year's results and a final summary volume similar to the University of Utah's descriptive Glen Canyon reports with their final interpretive volume after the close of the final season. The preliminary and descriptive nature of this report also holds true for the ecological data. Also in this regard, the Navajo archaeology will be discussed in a separate volume.

The above paragraph is not used as an excuse for temerity in speculation. In fact, I urge readers to speculate critically on our results and to convey their comments, criticisms, and suggestions to me. This is yet another reason for the publication of descriptive reports prior to the conclusion of the Black Mesa project.

These initial excavations by Prescott College on Black Mesa fall into the category of salvage archaeology, a facet of archaeological research which no longer needs a defense. Jesse Jennings' (1966) *Glen Canyon: A Summary* is adequate testimony to the value of salvage projects. In order, however, to derive the maximum information from a salvage operation, it is necessary to have adequate time to formulate problems for testing before excavation begins. Fortunately, sufficient time was available before the 1968 field session began so that some hypotheses could be developed. Furthermore, the prospect of returning to northeastern Black Mesa in future years is excellent so that long range problems can be explored and questions which arise during the analysis of the initial year's survey and excavation program can be investigated.

The history of the archaeological investigations on northern Black Mesa can, unfortunately, be easily summarized. The only formal excavations on the northeastern portion of the mesa were carried out in 1936 and 1937 by the famed Rainbow Bridge-Monument Valley expedition during which a single site was excavated and this was considered "somewhat outside the area most extensively studied . . ." by the expedition. Numerous archaeologists have traversed the area north to south (Watson Smith, personal communication), but only one or two sites have ever been formally recorded. Little explanation can be offered for this archaeological neglect, but it may well be due to the virtual absence of the scenic grandeur of the canyon country a few miles to the north of the mesa and the scarcity of the large dry caves which can produce such spectacular perishable material as the Basketmaker II and Pueblo III sites in the canyon country.

The prospect of excavating on Black Mesa is exciting because it is one of the few large areas in the Southwest which has seldom seen the archaeologist's shovel. As mentioned above, the only previous excavation on northern Black Mesa was carried out by the Rainbow Bridge-Monument Valley expedition when Watson Smith cleared RBMV 551 only four miles north of the area where Prescott College worked (Beals *et al.* 1945). Because of this paucity of excavation, archaeologists for years have pointed to Black Mesa as the source of all unanswered questions about the prehistory of surrounding regions (Brew 1946:302; Lindsay and Ambler 1963:91). It is the old refrain of the answers lying where there has been no excavation.

No pretext is made that survey and excavations on Black Mesa will answer even a small fraction of the numerous questions posed by archaeologists for the Anasazi country. Some of the major questions of cultural history we hope to shed some light on, however, are listed below:

1) What is the cultural affiliation of the archaeological remains on Black Mesa? Is it possible to distinguish cultural differences between the Kayenta-Marsh Pass region and the Hopi country, *i.e.*, between the Kayenta Branch and what Colton (1939) calls the Tusayan Branch? Is the Tusayan Branch and its various pottery types a meaningful regional variant?

2) If regional cultural variations are distinguishable, what are their distinctive features and why did these features become distinctive? A broader question is, what is the process in the development of a distinguishable regional tradition? What role does environment play in this development?

3) Were people living on Black Mesa since Archaic times or did people living in the Kayenta or Tusayan areas move onto the mesa in the centuries after Christ?

4) Black Mesa, the area between Kayenta-Marsh Pass and the Hopi region, was abandoned sometime between A.D. 1200 and the arrival of the Spanish. When? Why? Can site surveys distinguish a gradual abandonment of Black Mesa or was the entire area depopulated about the same time?

5) What is the cultural relationship of the prehistoric people living on Black Mesa to the Mesa Verde and Chaco Branches? Can any relationship be traced to the central Little Colorado Valley?

6) The pithouse has been demonstrated to be a common dwelling form for

the Kayenta Anasazi through the Pueblo III period. Is this the case on Black Mesa, and if so, what is the reason for the dual dwelling forms — surface structures and contemporaneous pithouses?

7) Preliminary reconnaissance indicates most of the Anasazi sites are small and scattered. Is there any evidence for inter-settlement cooperation, and if so, what is the nature of the cooperation?

8) Some recent studies have suggested that the Anasazi depended more on hunting and gathering than on agriculture. To what extent did hunting and gathering contribute to the food supply on Black Mesa? Furthermore, what are the natural edible resources on Black Mesa, and what is their distribution and density? Could the people on Black Mesa have utilized the wild plant and animal food to a greater extent than they did? Did the ratio of cultivated to non-cultivated food change through time?

9) The possibility that several Anasazi pottery types have differential distribution within a site due to functional rather than temporal differences has been suggested. The hypothesis that the intrasite distribution of pottery types is due to functional differences is to be tested on Black Mesa.

10) What is the nature of the Navajo occupation on Black Mesa? When was Black Mesa first occupied by Navajos, and was it a refuge area both after Spanish reprisals and during American harassment?

The above range of questions covers only a small band of the entire spectrum of concerns about prehistoric and historic man on Black Mesa — questions which have been asked since the early days in Southwestern archaeology, and which have become more important as the regions surrounding the mesa have seen more work. Obviously, at the conclusion of the first season's work numerous other questions can be posed and, hopefully as excavations continue, our original problems will develop into more sophisticated problems.

In the above emphasis on research and questions of culture history and to some extent culture process, I have not meant to denigrate another primary concern of the Black Mesa Project, and that is teaching. I have perhaps emphasized research in the above discussion because I hold that research and teaching are inseparable, *i.e.*, the instructor must also be a student and the student must also be a researcher.

The Black Mesa Project is operated as a field school. We have taken advantage of this so-called "salvage project" to train archaeologists. There is a trend today, it seems, to divide field schools into two types. The student either learns how to shovel dirt, or he learns how to develop and test hypotheses, and the more sophisticated and elegant the better.

The Prescott College field school program has three major goals. The first facet of the program is to teach the student how to shovel, to build up a storehouse of experience so that the student knows when to dig deeper, to take notes, to follow a wall, and to draw an accurate profile. This is the aspect of archaeology that involves "common sense," and when an individual has mastered these techniques he is said to have a good "field sense."

[3]

The second facet of the field school revolves around the concept of culture-history. What happened to whom on Black Mesa? Most of the questions posed above are problems of culture-history. Who were the inhabitants of Black Mesa; how did they live; why did they abandon northeastern Black Mesa, etc.? The advantage of Black Mesa as the region for the field school is that all individuals — students and teachers — are in a sense starting from scratch. Instructors have a better "field sense" developed through experience and perhaps a better grasp of Southwestern archaeological literature, but since the culture-history of Black Mesa is so poorly known, everyone is formulating ideas and as a group we are testing them. The student is not doing a chemistry or math problem that hundreds of thousands of students have performed before him but is developing original ideas and doing original research at an undergraduate level.

The third facet of the Prescott College field school is to formulate and test questions of culture process — in a sense the why of culture-history. Why, for example, do sub-cultures develop; what are the alternatives of subsistence in an upland arid environment and why are certain of the alternatives chosen in certain environments at certain levels of cultural complexity.

How are these three aspects of the field school being approached? Obviously, the teaching of archaeological techniques is accomplished both by reading and by explanation in the field as work progresses. In addition, many specialists such as dendrochronologists, biologists, geologists, and specialists in archaeomagnetism visit the camp and explain their methods and techniques of their sciences which are both ancillary to archaeology and an integral part of the discipline.

The questions of culture-history and process are initially formulated in camp in semi-formal discussions in the mess hall-lecture hall at a blackboard or the seemingly more stimulating influence of the very informal campfire dialogue. Outside of the jotting down of ideas and three and four page reports on problems of culture-history, little of the discussion is formally written up.

Little laboratory work is accomplished in the field. Sherds and stones are washed and materials sorted. After the field session is over, the gross laboratory work, *i.e.*, the typing of sherds and the cataloguing of artifacts, is done at Prescott College before the Fall Quarter begins.

During the Fall Quarter I hold a class in laboratory techniques. An advantage is that by the time classes start, the vast majority of what is usually taught in laboratory techniques courses is already accomplished and the students and instructors can get the written descriptive report out of the way and each student or a group of students can develop a problem and test it. What are the functions of worked sherds? Is the yellow pottery we are finding coal fired? What is the evidence for differing adaptations to the environment through time? It is at this level that the student is using the miniscule and often dull fact that he collected and testing the question he asked earlier in the summer. As more and more data are collected over the summers, the possibility of obtaining the correct answer becomes greater for all researchers.

[4]

CHAPTER TWO

The Environmental Setting

Physiography

BLACK MESA LIES WITHIN THE NAVAJO PORTION of the Colorado Plateau province in the northeast corner of Arizona (Fig. 1). The cap and encircling walls of the mesa are composed of Mesa Verde sandstone. Black Mesa, with a diameter of some 75 miles and a circumference of 275 miles, has often been described as a hand with the palm being the highest point to the northeast. The hand dips to the southwest with the fingers forming the Hopi Mesas which are the southern extensions of Black Mesa.

The Mesa Verde sandstone is buff or gray massive at the base and top with varying degrees of cross-bedding. Arenaceous and argillaceous shale and coal occur in beds of varying thickness. The Mesa Verde sandstone presents a relatively uniform appearance of rolling hills dissected by numerous washes most of which trend to the southwest. With the exception of the northern escarpment of Black Mesa, often as high as 1200 to 2000 feet above the surrounding plains and valleys, the sheer canyon walls typical of the Tsegi system to the north are absent. Consequently, the unsurpassed scenic grandeur of the brightly colored canyon systems to the north, the awesomeness of Monument Valley to the northeast, and the convoluted volcanic forms of the Hopi Buttes to the south are not present on Black Mesa.

Many of the small washes have cut deeply into the alluvium and debouch into the much larger Tusayan washes which have deeply incised the Mesa Verde sandstone. The westernmost Tusayan Wash, Moenkopi Wash, drains the entire northern and western areas of Black Mesa including the immediate area of study.

The elevation decreases from 8110 feet at the northeast edge of the mesa to approximately 6300 feet near the southwest edge. The terrain is rolling and there are no prominent peaks or mountains on the top of the mesa.

Alluvium and aeolian deposits are relatively thin on the mesa top. Large areas of sand dunes exist only near the southwestern edge where the predominantly southwest winds form large areas of cliff-head dunes. The alluvium in the large washes is often distinguishable in three well-developed terraces. Whether or not these three alluvial units correlate with the Jeddito, Tsegi, and Naha for-

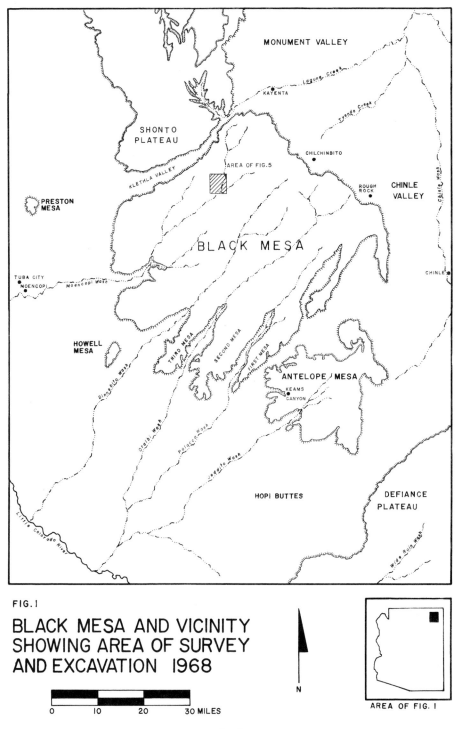

FIG. 1

BLACK MESA AND VICINITY SHOWING AREA OF SURVEY AND EXCAVATION 1968

0   10   20   30 MILES

N

AREA OF FIG. 1

[6]

FIGURE 2. *Northwestern flank of Black Mesa at its highest elevation.*

FIGURE 3. *Upper Moenkopi Wash. View is toward the northeast.*

mations, described for the southern section of Black Mesa (Hack 1942), has not as yet been determined.

Hydrography

There is no perennial stream in the entire geographic province. The largest wash in the study area, Moenkopi Wash, is dry most of the year. Usually, however, water is standing in pools in the bottom of the wash or can be obtained from digging shallow holes in the stream channel (Fig. 3). This situation also applies to Coal Mine Wash which is a major tributary to the north of Moenkopi Wash. As is typical in the arid Southwest, even the major washes carry large amounts of water only after heavy summer rainfall or after a quick thaw of heavy snow cover. The washes may discharge a tremendous amount of water but only for a short period. This pattern of long dry periods and then a short but rapid discharge is even more true for the innumerable small washes than it is for the larger drainage systems. Most of the small washes eventually drain into Moenkopi Wash, although some simply debouch their load of water and silt into low alluvial filled depressions.

Two seeps were noted in the Mesa Verde sandstone near the northeastern rim of the mesa, but no active or fossil seeps or springs were found in the excavated or surveyed regions. This absence of springs does not, of course, suggest that springs were not present prehistorically. The scarcity of ground water today, however, indicates that it was also scarce in the past.

Unlike the Navajo sandstone of Shonto Plateau to the north, the Mesa Verde sandstone does not form potholes and catchment areas where standing water can usually be found after rainstorms. As a result, the inhabitants of Black Mesa were denied this additional source of water. One advantage, however, is that Black Mesa lacks the large areas of slick rock because of the nature of the Mesa Verde sandstone and there is a great deal more soil for agriculture on the upland sections of Black Mesa than there is on the uplands of the Shonto Plateau.

Climate

The climate of northwestern Black Mesa is difficult to access because of the total absence of any weather records for the immediate region. Nevertheless, personal observation indicates the climate is not atypical for the arid Southwest at this altitude. The weather records at Kayenta and Keams Canyon, although only a few miles from the study area, cannot be applied to Black Mesa because of the great difference in elevation and the effect this large land mass has on the climate.

Summers range in temperature from warm to hot in spite of the relatively high elevation. Weather records kept at the field camp for two years during the months of June and July show a range in minimum temperature from 40° to 65° with a mean high of 87° for the months of June and July. No temperature records are available for winter months, but occasional visits we made to the mesa in winter are ample evidence of occasional bitter cold weather. Below zero readings are not uncommon in Kayenta. When the sun is shining and there is no wind, daytime winter temperatures can be quite pleasant.

Precipitation occurs mainly in late summer during the months of July and August with very little rainfall in winter, spring, and autumn. Most summer precipitation is in the form of local heavy convectional thundershowers which form over the strongly heated mesas. Most of the moisture in these summer storms comes from the Gulf of Mexico. Often the showers are severe, causing locally heavy flooding, and are preceded by strong winds carrying considerable amounts of sand. It was often observed that thunderheads and rainstorms would develop over Black Mesa and the Shonto Plateau to the north, but the intervening Klethla and Long House Valleys were clear of rain. The total precipitation for June and July in 1968 was .18 in. and in 1969 2.58 in. This great variation in precipitation is apparently not uncommon.

The weather records for Betatakin, at an elevation of 7286 feet, from 1944 to 1959 (*Climatological Data, Arizona and Utah — U. S. Department of the Commerce, Weather Bureau 1932–1969*) can be used as an indication of the climate on northeastern Black Mesa because of the similarity in elevation. It must be kept in mind, however, that the two regions are in different physiographic provinces and the climatic regimen is probably somewhat different.

TABLE 1. *Weather records from Betatakin, Navajo National Monument, Arizona, 1944–1959.*

	Maximum Temperature	Minimum Temperature	Precipitation	Snowfall
January	41.10	21.50	1.16	11.60
February	42.20	19.80	.65	9.10
March	48.80	24.60	.88	1.40
April	60.80	34.20	.67	.30
May	71.60	40.90	.35	—
June	80.70	49.10	.54	—
July	80.60	56.10	2.03	—
August	83.70	54.50	1.70	—
September	76.20	51.50	1.23	—
October	67.30	40.60	.45	—
November	51.20	27.40	.73	7.90
December	41.00	21.40	.62	7.10

Precipitation in winter is usually in the form of snow, although seldom more than a few inches and this usually melts quickly except along the north face of the mesa. Most of the winter storms are cold, dry, and advance from the northwest carrying much sand.

Flora and Fauna

Most of Black Mesa is in the Upper Sonoran life zone. The vegetation is dominated visually by piñon and juniper. The dense stands of piñon and juniper

FIGURE 4. *Upland environment. Dead sagebrush is in the foreground and piñon and juniper trees are on the knolls. Ariz. D:11:2 is on the tree-covered ridge in the center of the figure.*

along the north cliff give the mesa a dark cast when viewed from a distance, because of which the mesa got its name. In the study area, the piñon and juniper are usually found clustered on the slopes and along ridges, and the lower areas are free of the trees. Piñon is more prevalent than juniper. At higher elevations the piñon and juniper are so dense it is difficult to walk through, and juniper clearance programs are presently being practiced by the Bureau of Land Management.

Dense but localized stands of ponderosa pine (*Pinus ponderosa*) and Douglas fir (*Pseudotsuga menziesii*) grow in the canyons along the headwaters of the Moenkopi and Coal Mine Washes at the higher elevations near the northeast corner of the mesa. Along the major washes, which usually have large amounts of tamarisk (*Tamarix* sp.), there is an occasional lone cottonwood (*Populus* sp.).

Sage brush (*Artemisia tridentata*) is common, especially in alluvial filled depressions. Great amounts of sagebrush have died, apparently from overgrazing (Fig. 4). Wolf berry or squawberry (*Lycium pallidum*) is common on historic and prehistoric sites. Wolf berry is one of the best indicators of habitation sites because of its preference for disturbed soil with a high organic content.

Annual grasses such as sand dropseed (*Sporobolus cryptandrus*), Indian rice grass (*Oryzopsis hymenoides*), and blue grama (*Bouteloua gracili*) only partially cover the sand and soil surface. Cholla (*Opuntia whipplei*) and prickly pear (*Opuntia* sp.) cactus are rare.

Animal life is extremely scarce in the study area with the unfortunate exception of prairie rattlesnakes. Twenty-two prairie rattlesnakes were killed during the 1968 field season in camp, and near excavated and surveyed sites. Several species of the ubiquitous lizard were observed as well as numerous cottontail and jackrabbits. Surprisingly, no coyotes were seen or heard, nor were any other larger mammals.

The scarcity of animal life and the recent erosion and destruction of flora (large amounts of dead sagebrush) can probably be accounted for in large part to overgrazing. The large number of livestock grazed on northern Black Mesa has destroyed a great portion of the ground cover so that domesticated animals have successfully competed for browse with large wild animals. The destruction of the ground cover by overgrazing has also permitted the torrential summer rains to greatly erode the ground surface.

Present Land Use

Five Navajo extended families currently occupy the northeastern part of Black Mesa. The most obvious — and destructive — use of the land by these families is for the grazing of livestock. Sheep and goats are most common but some cattle are also grazed. All families have large herds of sheep and goats, but no specific figures are available. Undoubtedly, the raising of livestock is the greatest economic source for the study area.

Most of the families also raise small amounts of corn, pumpkins, or squash. The small agricultural plots are located either in a depression or low area where water drains after a storm or on the low alluvial terraces along the major washes. The small size of the plots indicates that agriculture provides only a small portion of the Navajo diet on Black Mesa.

The mesa is utilized by many Navajos in surrounding regions as a source of firewood. Calcium is dug out of pockets near the north end of the mesa to whiten wool, and hematite is mined and used as a red dye.

CHAPTER THREE

The Survey

History

THE PRIMARY PURPOSE OF THE ARCHAEOLOGICAL SURVEY was to provide a listing of archaeological stations which were in danger of being destroyed by the mining operations of Peabody Coal Company. The archaeological objective is to do an intensive survey in order to use the obtained information as a tool for answering the questions posed in the introduction to this report.

The survey was conducted at several different times, and is at present incomplete. Only a small portion of the entire area to be disturbed by mining has been inspected. The reconnaissance will continue during the summer of 1969.

The initial reconnaissance was accomplished on July 26–28, 1967, by R. C. Euler. The survey involved approximately the following areas: 100 miles of slurry pipeline right-of-way from the western boundary of the Navajo Reservation near Mesa Butte, trending northeasterly to a point on the upper interior portion of Black Mesa along the Moenkopi Wash; approximately 100 acres of the strip mine area; several miles of truck haulage road right-of-way; and approximately 100 acres of the proposed coal crushing plant site.

The slurry pipeline was surveyed entirely by helicopter and was later inspected by vehicle after trenching operations began. The strip mine areas, plant site, and truck haulage roads were also inspected from the helicopter and then in a four-wheel drive vehicle and on foot.

A second phase of the survey was undertaken on March 25, 1968, by Euler and Gumerman in the area of the proposed plant site. Peabody Coal Company indicated its desire to relocate the crushing plant, and consequently, the new location had to be surveyed. This inspection was done from a truck and on foot.

The third phase of the survey was undertaken at intermittent intervals during the six-weeks excavation program in June and July, 1968, as time and personnel permitted. The regions inspected during this period were in the initial strip mine areas. In addition, sites reported by the coal company personnel from other locations on the mesa were recorded at this time. This portion of the survey was carried out by a field school supervisor and two or more students. Occasionally, students surveyed in small groups after they had sufficient training.

A collection was made at all sites, including the recently abandoned Navajo sites. Each station, when discovered, was accorded a permanent site number in Prescott College's archaeological site survey which uses the quadrangle system. The letters (P.C.) are appended after each site number to distinguish the sites from those recorded by other institutions in Arizona. A standard Prescott College survey card was filled out for each site discovered, and a sketch was made of the site plan and location. In most cases, an aluminum tag, with the site number, was affixed to a rock or tree at the site. In the laboratory, the site card information was transferred to a 5 x 8 marginal punch card keyed for various attributes and the ceramic data collected on the survey added to the card. Plastic flagging tape was placed at the site and a coal company engineer located the site on the maps the company had prepared of the region.

Certainly, not all sites present in the surveyed area were located and recorded. The reconnaissance is, however, intensive rather than extensive and few sites probably escaped our attention. It is to be assumed that other evidence of human occupation will be discovered when excavation is undertaken in the surveyed regions.

For purposes of the survey, sites were identified on the basis of discrete concentrations of worked stone, sherds, or architecture. Navajo hogan clusters and corrals were recorded as single sites. Unlike many regions of the Southwest, there was no special difficulty in distinguishing the limits of an occupation zone or in determining if an extensive area of occupational debris should be recorded as more than one site. This is due to several factors: 1) The sites were small and scattered. There are few examples of dense concentrations of sites. 2) The processes of aggradation and degradation have been limited on northeastern Black Mesa relative to other areas of the Hopi and Navajo reservations. Consequently, evidence of human occupation has generally not been buried under great amounts of alluvium nor have the sites been unduly eroded, and cultural material scattered. 3) Most settlements appear to have been occupied for only a relatively short time and few can be considered double component sites. Those sites which are obviously double components have been counted as two sites in the enumeration of settlements with structures visible on the surface, in temporal span charts, and in several other figures. Therefore, in some enumeration of settlement characteristics, the number of sites may total more than fifty-six.

A total of fifty-six sites was recorded and given numbers Ariz. D:11:1 (P.C.) through Ariz. D:11:52 (P.C.), Ariz. D:7:1 (P.C.), Ariz. C:16:1 (P.C.), Ariz. I:3:1 (P.C.), and Ariz. I:3:2 (P.C.). The areal extent of the survey is shown in Figure 5. Five of the sites are situated slightly off the map and are not shown. Navajo settlements and Anasazi sites located on the slurry pipeline will be reported in a later publication.

All of the prehistoric sites are habitation sites. The prehistoric sites, totaling forty-one, are all assigned to the Kayenta Anasazi, and have a temporal span of late Basketmaker III to early Pueblo III. Of the eleven historic sites, ten are recent Navajo and one is an abandoned Anglo trading post.

Site Distribution and Environmental Situation

The initial survey program was limited in areal extent and in the time devoted to it. Therefore, statements concerning settlement patterns on northeastern Black Mesa must be tentative because of the limited sample. The surveys of the strip mine areas and the coal preparation plant location are the only ones that can give an accurate picture of the site distribution. The surveys of road, powerline, and waterline right-of-ways are linear rather than areal in scope although the information garnered on these surveys has added considerably to the data.

Settlement patterns were determined by soil and water conditions, and probably also by a changing economic adaptation to the environment.

There is the suggestion of a change in environmental situation for habitation sites which developed between Basketmaker III and early Pueblo III. The single late Basketmaker III and the seven sites through late Pueblo I, with one exception, are all situated on the first major terrace of the upper Moenkopi Wash. The later sites are more often found in the broad open rolling upland region. Navajo sites are found in both environmental situations. The change in settlement location may be a function of a change in the subsistence economy, both in a shift in emphasis from a collecting economy to an agricultural economy and also a shift in agricultural techniques.

The evidence from excavation suggests that the people living on Black Mesa depended heavily on domesticated crops as a food source, and since the sites are small, it can be assumed that the habitation sites were situated near the fields. It would appear, therefore, that during the late Basketmaker III and Pueblo I periods, the flood plain along the Moenkopi Wash was utilized for agriculture and that the primary mode of cultivation was flood water farming. During the late Pueblo II and Pueblo III periods, the emphasis was on dry farming in the upland area. The many small dune depressions and small alluvial filled swales and valleys provided the bulk of cultivated land. Both of these environmental situations are exploited by the Navajo today, although there seems to be a preference for corn production on the flood plain of the Moenkopi Wash and for squash in the uplands.

The apparent shift from an emphasis on flood water farming to dry farming is easily documented but the reason for this shift is more difficult to explain. Numerous explanations have been advanced recently to explain the shift from the relatively well-watered river valleys in Basketmaker III and Pueblo I stages to the drier uplands beginning in late Pueblo II times. A shift in rainfall pattern or an increase in effective moisture has been postulated (Baerreis and Bryson 1965) or the opposite — a less favorable environment necessitating population movement for maintenance of the agricultural economy (Schoenwetter and Dittert 1968:52). Jennings (1966:55) has suggested improved or drought resistant strains of crops may have permitted the emphasis on dry farming in the more arid regions. This movement might have been dictated by population pressure in the better watered river valleys caused by an increased proficiency in the utilization

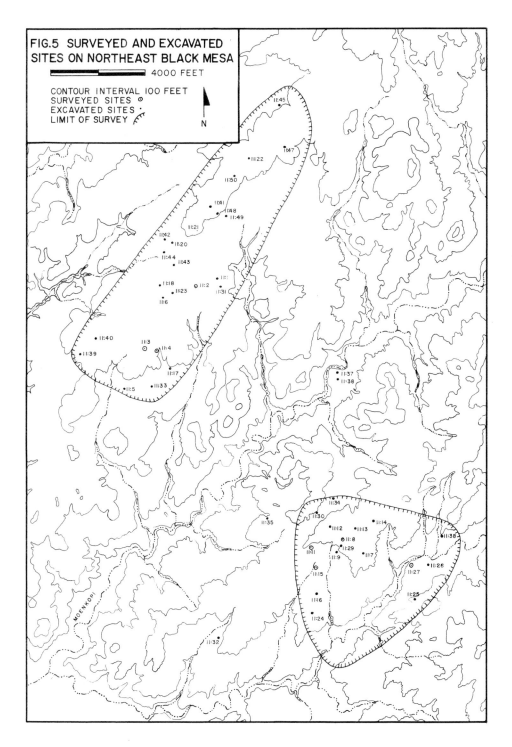

FIG.5 SURVEYED AND EXCAVATED
SITES ON NORTHEAST BLACK MESA

4000 FEET

CONTOUR INTERVAL 100 FEET
SURVEYED SITES ⊙
EXCAVATED SITES ·
LIMIT OF SURVEY

N

of water resources (Gumerman 1969:366–67). In any case, there does seem to be some sort of climate change in the A.D. 1050–1150 period and the other suggested causes above are not incompatible with this hypothesis. Obviously other factors not suggested may also have been the motivating force behind the shift in farming techniques and settlement patterns. Perhaps fossil pollen and soil studies may be the resolving element in this discussion.

Typically, the habitation sites lie on the elevations, however slight, above the surrounding terrain. Nevertheless, they are usually not situated at the crest of the elevation as is common throughout most of the Anasazi district, but rather they lie somewhat down on the slope, often on the leeward side. The preference for construction on the slope may be both for protection against the strong southwestern wind and also to avoid the bedrock, which is much closer to the surface or actually outcropping on the crest of the elevation. The excavated sites Ariz. D:11:3 and Ariz. D:11:11 are good examples of site locations on slopes, and Ariz. D:11:2 illustrates construction on the crest of an elevation.

Generally, the more precipitous and dissected areas were shunned as habitation sites. Regions with a shallow soil cover or large areas bare of soil were also not utilized for habitation. The J-27 strip (Fig. 1) area in which only a single prehistoric site was found illustrates this type of environmental situation. The terrain of the J-27 strip area is not extremely rugged, but is characterized by a lack of soil cover in many areas and by numerous sandstone outcrops. The sandstone in most cases has exfoliated in small pieces and often washed over the thin soil deposits in the low elevations. As a result, the region is unsuitable both for dwellings and agriculture.

Natural resources vary greatly in their occurrence. No existing springs were found on the survey, nor were areas which look especially likely to have springs in a slightly wetter regime. All sites are located near arable land in the form of either alluvial filled depressions and flats, or near the flood plain of Moenkopi Wash. Sandstone for masonry construction is available everywhere, either in large block form or in tabular fracturing sections. Chert and quartzite pebbles and cobbles suitable for the production of chipped stone tools are absent on Black Mesa and either the tools or raw material had to be imported. Clay for the construction of pottery vessels is present in pockets overlying the Mesa Verde sandstone and underlying the alluvium. Only small lenses of clay were found in the alluvial deposits themselves. Pink siltstone pebbles are common in the beds of the major washes and were commonly ground and utilized for personal ornaments.

No correlation can be made between natural resources and the topographical situation of the communities. It is customary to classify sites into several types according to their topographical situation, such as open sites, slump-boulder sites, rock shelter sites, and others. Relief is low and there are few precipitous cliffs and large slump-blocks in the study area, even along the major washes. As a result, all the sites can be classified as "open sites" as there are no structures built against protecting cliffs. Several cliff dwellings were observed near the extreme northeast end of the mesa, well outside the surveyed area.

Although there are obvious differences in the surface appearance of sites, all recorded Anasazi stations are considered habitation sites. The common term "campsite" was not used even for a small scattering of sherds because these areas were discovered to be the refuse from the occupation of numerous jacal structures. Sites without masonry or kiva depressions and a low number of sherds were given the non-committal title of "sherd areas."

Prehistoric trails or foot and hand holes pecked in sandstone cliffs were not found on the survey. This is due to the low relief on the mesa top which makes foot travel relatively easy.

No pictographs or petroglyphs were found anywhere on Black Mesa. This is most likely a result of the relatively loosely consolidated sandstone cliffs on which it would be difficult to peck or paint a design. Furthermore, few of the sandstone faces have developed a desert varnish which makes a suitable surface for rock art.

No indication of water or soil control systems was found on the survey, although an intensive search was made for check dams, agricultural plots, and irrigation ditches.

Architecture and Site Size

Determination of architectural patterns from surface indications is notoriously difficult even in a culture area so well-known as the Anasazi region. The frequency of the error of our guesses was emphasized once excavation was undertaken. The greatest errors were due to our underestimation of the number of jacal and ramada structures we would encounter and consequently, we often grossly underestimated the number of dwellings at individual sites. As yet, there is no satisfactory means of estimating the number of rooms constructed of perishable material at a site, except to say that undoubtedly there were some. For example, at Ariz. D:11:3 there was a single jacal structure, and at Ariz. D:11:14 (excavated in Autumn 1969) there were twenty-three jacal structures. Both of these sites were originally estimated to have two or three surface masonry rooms and a kiva, but Ariz. D:11:3 was thought to be larger because there was a greater amount of refuse visible on the surface. There appears to be no chronological significance to the presence of jacal structures since they occur at excavated sites of all periods from early Basketmaker III (excavated in the 1969 season) through early Pueblo III. Because of the impossibility of estimating the number of perishable structures at a site, the probable presence of these buildings at *all* sites will not be mentioned below. It should be remembered, however, that the sites are much larger than they appear or are reported because of this common architectural feature. It should also be noted here that semisubterranean mealing rooms are never revealed at the surface by depressions as are the kivas. They are, nevertheless, a consistent feature of the late Pueblo II and early Pueblo III sites on northeastern Black Mesa.

Ignoring, at present, the vexing problem of jacal structures, there is a definite similarity in architectural pattern. The deviation from the pattern is so slight that an architectural typology is not necessary. There is also a similarity in size. All the sites can be categorized as small. The largest site was recorded as having "ten-plus rooms" and the smallest as being a "sherd area." There does not appear to be any increase in size from Basketmaker III-Pueblo I to early Pueblo III, since Basketmaker III-Pueblo I villages are among the largest habitation sites recorded. All sites are in exposed locations and as mentioned above, no rockshelters or caves were recorded.

Evidence of architecture is visible at all except fourteen sites and it is of interest that these fourteen sites all belong to the latest period represented on the northeastern part of the mesa — late Pueblo II through early Pueblo III.

The earliest sites, Basketmaker III-Pueblo I through early Pueblo II, are all characterized by upright slabs or low mounds of sandstone slabs in disarray suggesting contiguous slab-lined storage cists. Often to the east or northeast of these slabs are one or several depressions indicating pithouses. The trash may be either to the northeast of the depression and storage cists or it may be sheet trash encompassing the entire site. In no case was coursed masonry observed at sites earlier than late Pueblo II.

The majority of late Pueblo II-early Pueblo III sites are characterized by no visible architecture on the surface and no kiva depressions (fourteen sites). It was assumed that the larger of these sites at least (usually called "sherd areas"), consist of pithouses or jacal structures. In five cases a depression which is assumed to indicate a kiva is associated with the sherd areas. Ten early Pueblo III sites have two or three masonry rooms visible on the surface all but three of which are associated with kiva depressions. Two of the sites have what appears to be vertical sandstone slab wall structures. In one instance, two kiva depressions were found at a site with at least four masonry rooms on the surface.

In most cases the orientation of the site is typically Anasazi, *i.e.*, masonry rooms with the kiva depression to the northeast or east between the trash midden and the masonry rooms. The rubble at one site suggested a U-shaped pueblo of ten or more rooms with a kiva depression in the center. This site as well as the excavated Ariz. D:11:3 were the only two late sites with outlying single room storage units.

The masonry at all the sites was relatively poorly constructed of Mesa Verde sandstone despite the fact that the local sandstone splits into blocks along rectangular planes of cleavage. Little dressing was needed to make the blocks suitable for house construction, and yet there was apparently little desire to select well-fitting sandstone blocks or slabs. In most instances, only small portions of wall were observed and no mortar was noted. If anything, the typical Black Mesa masonry was of slightly poorer quality than the traditionally inferior Kayenta workmanship.

In summary, the Basketmaker III through early Pueblo II architecture is typically of slab-lined surface cists and pithouses. The most common later site is the sherd area and small masonry pueblo with a kiva depression. All the sites are surprisingly small with three masonry rooms visible on the surface being the most common.

[18]

It must be emphasized that an extremely skewed picture is obtained by traditional survey techniques because of the prevalence of the jacal structure which is not visible on the surface. It will be only after considerable excavation is undertaken in the study area that we will be able to generalize about a site by looking at it prior to excavation.

Artifacts

Lithic Material

The only common source of raw material for stone artifacts is the Mesa Verde sandstone. Siltstone pebbles found in washes and as nodules in the sandstone were often ground into pendants. Chipped stone, an exotic material, is extremely scarce and even waste flakes are rare. The vast majority of stone tools were for the preparing of plant foods.

The terminology for stone tool description is taken mainly from Woodbury (1954), the exception being the substitution of the term pecking stone for pebble pounder. Chipped stone terminology is adapted from Haury (1950) and White (1963).

Chipped Stone

The incidence of chipped stone collected on survey and during excavation is virtually nil and is obviously the result of the absence of raw materials for the production of these artifacts. The Mesa Verde sandstone does not contain any intrusive rocks suitable for chipping. The nearest sources of raw material for chipped stone are the gravel covered terraces along the Colorado and San Juan Rivers. Chipped stone material in spite of its rareness is the most common intrusive item in both surveyed and excavated sites. It is doubtful that there has been much previous collecting on Black Mesa to account for the lack of chipped stone artifacts.

No temporal or cultural affiliation can be attributed to the chipped stone artifacts because of the smallness of the sample and the restricted temporal span of the collection.

A single *projectile point* unassociated with a site (Fig. 23, C) was collected from the surface on the last day of the survey. The point is white chert with a slightly convex expanding base. Part of one tang and part of the base is broken off. The point is 2 cm. long and 1.5 cm. wide. Two pieces of chert which show use scars along one edge were picked up from as many sites. These are miscellaneous *waste flakes* which appear to have been utilized for cutting or scraping. The flakes were not struck off of a prepared core and there is no retouching of the flake. One or two waste flakes were recovered from only six sites. A single site, Ariz. D:11:31, produced several hundred waste flakes of gray chert. All these flakes were of the same material and may have come from the same core. No significance can be attached to the fact that Ariz. D:11:31 is one of the few Pueblo I sites recorded.

Ground Stone

Ground stone artifacts, utilizing all local materials, are much more common than chipped stone artifacts. Utilitarian objects, such as manos, are all made of Mesa Verde sandstone. Smaller pieces of ground stone, probably used for ornaments, are produced from a pink-red siltstone found in the major washes in Black Mesa.

Manos (Fig. 24) comprise the single largest category of artifacts collected on the surface. Eighteen manos were found at fourteen sites. All of the grinding implements are two-handed or are too fragmentary to identify. Eight of the manos have two use surfaces, and all but three are flat, indicating their use on a flat metate. One mano has a finger grip along the leading edge. A fragmentary mano is stained red from the grinding of pigment. The maximum length is 21 cm. and the minimum is 12 cm. The maximum width is 11 cm. and the minimum is 7 cm. All manos are constructed of fine to medium grained sandstone. Three pieces of coarse grain ground sandstone appear to be *metate* fragments. All of these irregular-shaped pieces have one edge chipped-to-shape indicating that if they are metate fragments, they are of the flat variety.

One pink-red sub-rectangular siltstone *pendant* was found at Ariz. D:11:18, an early Pueblo II site. The edges and both surfaces have been smoothed by grinding. The beginning of a hole was drilled near one edge causing a small piece of the pendant to break and the presumed discarding of the artifact. The pendant is 3.2 cm. long and 2.7 cm. wide. Three *hammerstones* were found at three sites. All are unmodified fist-sized cobbles which show battering on two edges. One is quartzite and two are petrified wood, all imported materials on Black Mesa. Two pieces of *hematite* were found on as many sites. Both pieces of pigment evidence several facets from grinding.

Ceramics

Potsherds were collected from all the Anasazi sites, the number of sherds from individual sites ranging from two to more than one hundred. A total of 1,325 sherds was recovered from the survey alone (Table 2). All sherds were grouped into previously described wares and types (Fig. 6 and 7). The major sources for type descriptions were Colton and Hargrave (1937) and Colton (1955, 1956). Various refinements in Kayenta ceramics detailed in the numerous publications resulting from the Glen Canyon excavations were also taken into account.

Surprisingly not a single intrusive sherd was found either on the survey or in excavated sites (unless Abajo Red-on-orange is considered intrusive) in spite of the fact that a diligent search was made for trade pottery. The lack of intrusive sherds allows a simple presentation of the ceramic picture.

The decorated pottery is mainly Tusayan White Ware, with the most common types being by Sosi and Dogoszhi Black-on-white numbering 222 and 126 sherds respectively. Black Mesa Black-on-white runs a close third with 103 recorded. Sherds which have all the characteristics of a white ware but no

FIGURE 6. *White Ware type sherds from survey and excavation. A, B, C, Kana-a Black-on-white; D, E, F, G, Black Mesa Black-on-white; H, I, J, K, L, Sosi Black-on-white; M, N, O, Dogoszhi Black-on-white; P, Q, Flagstaff Black-on-white.*

TABLE 2. *Occurrence of pottery types at surveyed sites.*

Type	Ariz. D:11:2	Ariz. D:11:3	Ariz. D:11:4	Ariz. D:11:7	Ariz. D:11:8	Ariz. D:11:9	Ariz. D:11:10	Ariz. D:11:11	Ariz. D:11:12	Ariz. D:11:13	Ariz. D:11:14	Ariz. D:11:15	Ariz. D:11:16	Ariz. D:11:17	Ariz. D:11:18	Ariz. D:11:19	Ariz. D:11:20	Ariz. D:11:21
Tusayan White Ware	X	X		X	X			X				X		X	X	X		X
Lino B/G							X											
Kana-a B/W				X	X										X			
Black Mesa B/W	X	X			X	X		X	X	X		X		X	X	X		
Sosi B/W	X	X		X	X	X		X	X	X	X		X	X	X	X	X	X
Dogoszhi B/W	X	X	X		X			X	X	X	X		X	X		X	X	X
Flagstaff B/W		X	X		X			X	X	X	X	X	X	X		X		
Shato Variety	X							X						X				
Unclassified B/W		X			X	X			X						X	X	X	X
Abajo R/O						X												
Tusayan Gray Ware	X				X	X		X						X	X			X
Coconino Gray		X			X													
Kana-a Gray					X		X								X			
Lino Gray							X											
Lino Tradition							X									X		
Honani Tooled	X								X									
O'Leary Tooled								X										
Tusayan Corrugated	X	X		X	X	X		X	X	X	X	X		X	X	X	X	X
Moenkopi Corrugated	X	X	X		X			X	X		X		X	X		X	X	X
Kiet Siel Gray																		
Tsegi Orange Ware	X				X	X		X					X			X		
Medicine B/R					X				X									
Tusayan B/R	X			X		X		X				X	X			X	X	
Tsegi R/O																		
Deadmans B/R		X																
Tusayan Polychrome	X							X								X		X
Polacca Polychrome			X															
San Juan Red Ware		X			X		X				X							

TABLE 2. *Occurrence of pottery types at surveyed sites.*

Ariz. D:11:22	Ariz. D:11:23	Ariz. D:11:24	Ariz. D:11:25	Ariz. D:11:26	Ariz. D:11:27	Ariz. D:11:28	Ariz. D:11:30	Ariz. D:11:31	Ariz. D:11:32	Ariz. D:11:33	Ariz. D:11:35	Ariz. D:11:37	Ariz. D:11:38	Ariz. D:11:42	Ariz. D:11:43	Ariz. D:11:44	Ariz. D:11:45	Ariz. D:11:46	Ariz. D:11:47	Ariz. D:11:49	Ariz. D:11:50	Ariz. D:11:51	Ariz. D:11:52
X	X	X	X	X	X	X	X			X			X	X	X	X			X	X	X	X	X
			X	X	X				X		X	X											
X	X	X			X	X	X			X			X			X	X		X	X	X		
X	X	X	X	X	X	X	X		X	X	X		X	X	X	X	X			X	X	X	X
X	X	X	X			X	X			X			X	X	X		X			X			X
	X	X					X						X	X		X							
X	X						X								X								
X	X	X	X	X			X			X	X		X	X	X	X	X			X	X		X
	X	X	X			X	X	X				X							X				
				X	X			X				X	X										
	X						X	X				X							X				
X	X	X	X	X			X	X	X	X	X	X	X	X	X	X	X	X		X			X
X	X	X		X	X		X			X										X			
			X																				
	X	X	X		X	X				X	X					X	X	X	X	X			X
																							X
X	X	X	X	X		X	X			X				X						X			
	X																						
X	X	X										X		X						X			

painted decoration have been classified as Tusayan White Ware. These are probably either body sherds of decorated vessels or fragments of undecorated Tusayan White Ware vessels. White ware pieces with an unusual design or a design element too small to be classified are placed in the category Tusayan White Ware under the rubric "unidentified." Shato Black-on-white has been treated as a variant. Decorated bowls with a corrugated exterior have been typed by a traditionally recognized design style and then it was noted that the exterior was corrugated, i.e., Shato Variety.

Tusayan Gray Ware is dominated by Tusayan Corrugated (Fig. 10, A and B). Body sherds, of what has traditionally been called Lino Gray, have been placed in the Lino Tradition category (Ambler et al. 1964:73) because of the impossibility of distinguishing body sherds of Lino Gray from Kana-a Gray. Sherds which are classifiable as to ware but not as to type are simply recorded as Tusayan Gray Ware.

A plate-like form of Tusayan Gray Ware, tentatively called Tsegi Corrugated (Lindsay, personal communication), is common in excavated sites (Fig. 9, A and B). The plates which are dish-shaped are relatively crude with a typical Tusayan Gray Ware interior. The exterior surface ranges from crude indented corrugations and large unindented coils, to roughly obliterated coils. Rarely the rim was perforated while the clay was still wet. A separate study, as to function and distribution of this type, is now being done.

Tsegi Orange Ware forms the final major category. Tusayan Black-on-red is the most common type followed by Medicine Black-on-red. The temporal range of the sites on Black Mesa is too early to have any polychromes represented except for a small scattering of Tusayan Polychrome. As with the white wares, orange ware without decoration is classified as Tsegi Orange Ware and those pieces with painted elements too small to be identfied are placed under the rubric "unidentified" in the Tsegi Orange Ware column. The high percentage of sherds, classified simply as Tsegi Orange Ware, does not indicate a lesser amount of painted decoration on this ware. It is more a reflection of the characteristic of the surface of Tsegi Orange Ware vessels to exfoliate and the black paint to fade.

Eight sherds which fit the type description of Abajo Black-on-orange were found at Ariz. D:11:10, a late Basketmaker III-Pueblo I site on Moenkopi Wash. Whether these are from locally manufactured vessels or from trade pieces from the north is not known.

The single consistent variation to Kayenta pottery types is a small percentage of Tusayan White Ware and Tusayan Gray Ware which has a yellowish cast. The yellow, which is on the undecorated portions of the painted vessels and covers the entire area of the plain vessels, varies from a very pale yellow to a deep yellow-orange. The decorated portions of the vessels, which have the traditional designs of Pueblo II and III white wares, vary from black on the lighter yellow vessels to a very deep brown-orange on the yellow-orange vessels. Often the decoration is slightly glazed or there is only a "ghost" pattern remaining.

The yellow cast to the pottery, which is similar to the range in color of Hopi

FIGURE 7. *Orange Ware and Polychrome type sherds from survey and excavation. A, Abajo Red-on-orange; B, C, Tusayan Black-on-red; D, E, Medicine Black-on-red; F, G, Tusayan Polychrome.*

FIGURE 8. *White and Orange ware vessels. A, Medicine Black-on-red; B, Tusayan Polychrome; C, Tusayan White Ware; D, Dogoszhi Black-on-white; E, Sosi Black-on white; F, G, Black Mesa Black-on-white. Diameter of E, 22.5 cm.*

A   B

C   D   E   F

FIGURE 9. *Miniature vessels and gray ware plates. A, B, exterior of gray ware plates; C, D, E, miniature Tusayan White Ware vessels; F, miniature Tsegi Orange Ware vessel. Maximum diameter of E, 6.4 cm.*

A   B   C

FIGURE 10. *Large jars from excavated sites. A, B, Tusayan Corrugated; C, Dogoszhi Black-on-white. Height of C, 45 cm.*

Pueblo IV and V, appears to be due to an overfiring, perhaps due to the use of coal as fuel. The change to a yellow cast pottery in the Pueblo IV period has often been attributed to a switch from wood to coal for firing the vessels. The coal outcrops apparent all over northeastern Black Mesa may well have been utilized as a fuel soon after the Anasazi occupation of this upland. A detailed study of the problem of coal-fired pottery is planned for a later volume.

Chronology and Population Patterns

Compared to the rest of the New World, the American Southwest, especially the Anasazi area, has the advantage of precise dating techniques and a fairly secure chronology. Nevertheless, for many questions of culture-history and culture process, a refinement of chronology greater than can be derived from a surface survey is necessary. As a result, one of the major aims of the Black Mesa program is to excavate all the sites in a small drainage. In this way, utilizing tree-ring dating and archeomagnetic dating, it should be possible to determine more exactly relative and absolute dates and the possible contemporaneity of various sites. Too often archaeologists assume sites are contemporaneous because their ceramic assemblages are roughly similar. Some ceramic assemblages last for several centuries and none of the sites in a particular area, with these ceramic assemblages, may be contemporaneous. The question of contemporaneity has important consequences in such questions as population patterns and inter-site relationships.

The chronological positioning of surveyed sites on Black Mesa is difficult to determine in spite of the excellent tree-ring chronology for the Kayenta area. Tree-ring specimens from excavated sites have been submitted to the Laboratory of Tree-ring Research at the University of Arizona, but as of this date, the results have not been received.

Architectural variation in surveyed sites is not an accurate reflection of relative dates on Black Mesa because of the large number of sites with no visible architecture which range from late Basketmaker III through early Pueblo III. Chipped and ground stone artifacts similarly cannot be used for dating because of the virtual absence of chipped stone and the ground stone artifacts are temporally undiagnostic. As a result, the burden of dating falls to the old Southwestern standby — ceramics.

Most decorated pottery types of the Kayenta Anasazi have been found numerous times in association with datable tree-ring specimens (Breternitz 1966; Bannister et al. 1968), so that some gross temporal placement can be assigned to the majority of survey sites. Seriation would be an ideal tool for the relative dating of individual sites because of the association of these pottery types with dated tree-ring specimens. The small size of most of the sites and the concomitant small size of the sherd collection makes seriation in this instance a statistically unreliable tool. It will be necessary, therefore, to select the more chronologically sensitive sherds in each of the larger collections in making an estimation of the sites' chronological position. The dates assigned to the sites are largely based on the scheme of Breternitz (1966).

[28]

To facilitate the relative temporal placement of sites, individual pottery types have been grouped into commonly occurring complexes shown in Table 3 as has been done by Colton (1953:65–6). Only those types which are known to be relatively sensitive chronological indicators are used. After the ceramic complexes were established they were assigned to various periods in the traditional Pecos Classification. I feel that during the initial season of survey and excavation, the archaeology of Black Mesa was still sufficiently unknown to warrant not using the phase system devised by Colton (1939) for the Kayenta Anasazi. The correspondence of ceramic complexes with the Pecos Classification is shown in Table 4.

The decorated pottery types of the Kayenta Anasazi form a design style continuum (Beals *et al.* 1945), and consequently it is often difficult to place a particular sherd in a specific category within the stylistic evolutionary sequence. As a result of this stylistic gradation, many sites have ceramic assemblages which overlap several periods. I have, therefore, designated transitional stages, such as Pueblo I-II, to account for this gradation from one stage to another. If only a very small percentage of sherds belong to an earlier or later period than the great

TABLE 3. *Complexes of commonly occurring temporally diagnostic pottery types from Black Mesa.*

Complex A	Lino Black-on-gray Lino Gray	Complex E	Black Mesa Black-on-white Tusayan Corrugated
Complex B	Lino Black-on-gray Kana-a Black-on-white Lino Gray Kana-a Gray	Complex F	Black Mesa Black-on-white Sosi Black-on-white Dogoszhi Black-on-white Flagstaff Black-on-white Tusayan Corrugated and other Gray Ware
Complex C	Kana-a Black-on-white Kana-a Gray		
Complex D	Kana-a Black-on-white Black Mesa Black-on-white Kana-a Gray Tusayan Corrugated	Complex G	Sosi Black-on-white Dogoszhi Black-on-white Flagstaff Black-on-white Tusayan Corrugated and other Gray Ware

TABLE 4. *Correlation of pottery complexes with the Pecos Classification.*

Complex A	Basketmaker III	Complex E	Pueblo II

Complex B	Late Basketmaker III-
	    Early Pueblo I
		Complex F	Late Pueblo II-Early
			    Pueblo III

Complex C	Pueblo I	Complex G	Pueblo III
Complex D	Late Pueblo I-Early Pueblo II		

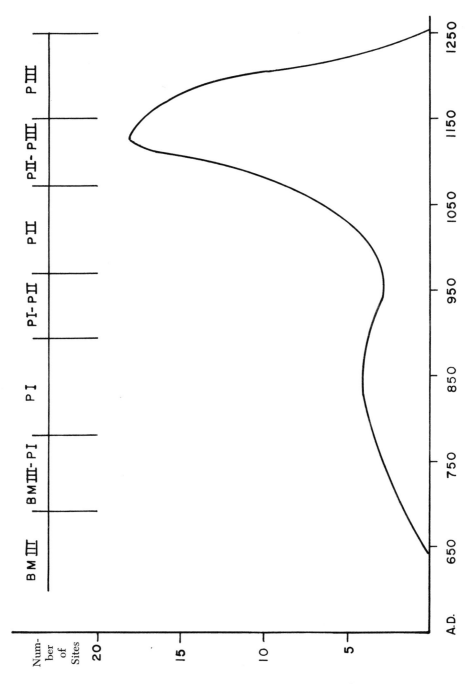

FIGURE 11. *Temporal distribution of surveyed sites.*

majority of the collection, the site is placed in the period in which the majority of sherds belong. If the collection, however, is obviously from a two component site, it is tabulated as two separate settlements for the tabulation of temporal site distribution. The collections from five sites were too small to accurately assign a temporal designation to the occupations and the sites were therefore not counted in the chronological designation of sites.

The temporal distribution of surveyed sites has a familiar pattern in Anasazi culture-history. A frequency polygon (Fig. 11) shows the distribution of surveyed sites through time beginning with a single Basketmaker III-Pueblo I site and increasing to four during the Pueblo I period. There is a slight decline to three in the Pueblo I-II period and then an increase to four during Pueblo II. This slight shift in the number of sites from Pueblo I-II to Pueblo II is probably due to the small sample rather than a culturally significant factor. There is a great increase in the number of sites during the Pueblo II-III period to eighteen and then a decrease to eleven in Pueblo III.

The Pecos Classification, although usually used as a cultural rather than a temporal scheme, is often assigned dates for each stage. Rough dates are assigned in Figure 11 to each stage with the realization that as yet no tree-ring specimens have been processed and that for the Glen Canyon region (Ambler *et al.* 1964; Lindsay *et al.* 1968) and the Laguna Creek area (Bannister *et al.* 1968:64–5), there has been an upward extension of dates.

Certainly northeastern Black Mesa was occupied prior to the late Basketmaker III-early Pueblo I period (several early Basketmaker III sites were excavated during the 1969 field season). The only indication of a pre-ceramic horizon on Black Mesa is a Pinto projectile point collected on the surface by the wife of a Navajo laborer. In any case, a permanent occupation that increases relatively regularly begins about A.D. 650. The tremendous increase in the number of sites beginning about A.D. 1050 is common throughout the drier upland areas of the Anasazi Southwest. The increase in habitation sites has been noted in such places as the Kaiparowitz Plateau (Fowler and Aikens 1963), Walhalla Glades (Hall 1942), Wetherill Mesa (Hayes 1964), the Shonto Plateau (Anderson 1969) and the Hopi Buttes (Gumerman and Skinner 1968). The depopulation of many of these areas also corresponds to the depopulation of Black Mesa about A.D. 1200. The mesa was then probably not again permanently inhabited until the Navajo occupation at an as yet undetermined time. Little will be said in this report concerning the reasons for this population fluctuation because these will be discussed in a subsequent volume.

The frequency of sites, as a key to population fluctuations, is an inaccurate but not totally unsuitable method, since, as was mentioned in the section on site size, there is little apparent difference in settlement size from period to period. As a result, the fluctuation in the number of sites reflects the fluctuations in population on the mesa.

CHAPTER FOUR

Excavations

EXCAVATION METHODS FOLLOWED, in general, the typical Southwestern style, although modification of technique was necessary late in the season as will be discussed below.

Where masonry was visible, trenches were put in at right angles to suspected walls. When the walls were reached, the exterior walls of the room block were cleared. Then room interiors were excavated, dividing the materials into fill and floor fill. If roofing debris was discernable, as it was in a few cases, all material below the roof was called floor fill. Only if an artifact was resting directly on the floor was the provenience designated floor. In most cases, roofing materials could not be distinguished and an arbitrary 7 to 12 cm. above floor was called floor fill.

At all sites where there was a kiva, a depression was visible making a determination of the kiva limits relatively simple. A trench was placed through the depression and once the walls were found they were traced by shovel and trowel. The cental portion of the kiva fill was then removed by backhoe.

At all excavated sites, test trenches were put in by hand or with a backhoe to test for subsurface structures. A definite pattern involving the subsurface mealing room north and east of the kiva was revealed in this manner. No pithouses were discovered, however.

A problem developed with the discovery of the numerous jacal or ramada structures. With only one or two postholes to suggest a structure of perishable material, how could the excavations be expanded to search for a posthole pattern and yet maintain some degree of horizontal control? Since the settlements were all obviously single component sites, we decided not to use a simple grid system but instead designate certain likely looking areas to be excavated by letter and called them strip areas. Once a structure was found within a strip area, however, the strip area designation was abandoned and a structure number was assigned. This system did not prove totally satisfactory because horizontal control was poor and the system was modified during the 1969 season.

A one meter square grid system was set up over the trash area at Ariz. D:11:3 to provide better control, especially of the squares which were screened. At other sites, however, the trash was simply test trenched. In most cases, except where mentioned in the individual site description, fill from trash areas, test trenches, and rooms was not screened.

Excavation involving detail work, most of the mapping, and note taking was done by the students with the help of the supervisory staff. Backfilling, test trenching, and the onerous, but necessary, task of moving dirt from one pile to another was done by the Navajo laborers.

Two types of heavy equipment were used. A tractor-backhoe was employed to remove the fill from kivas and to test for subsurface structures. In several instances, the backhoe bucket was placed into a deep kiva and loose dirt was hand shoveled into it to eliminate the long throw of dirt from the bottom of the kiva. At Ariz. D:11:15, a road grader was used to strip areas a few inches at a time in order to discover posthole patterns or subsurface structures. The use of the road grader was justified by the press of time. Ariz. D:11:15 was excavated during the school year and only a limited amount of time could be devoted to it. The effectiveness of the road grader varied with the operator. At Ariz. D:11:15 and Ariz. D:11:12 (excavated in the summer of 1969) a skilled operator was able to peel very cleanly a few centimeters of overburden off at each pass. Sterile soil was easily distinguishable from fill. At Ariz. D:11:23 (a 1969 excavation) an unskilled operator certainly destroyed more than he revealed.

Notes were taken in several ways. Standardized forms, for such features as room and burial descriptions, were used for uniformity and simplicity. All sherds and artifacts were saved and are on repository at Prescott College as are all notes and tabulation of data. Amplification of these forms and information not easily transcribable into forms were taken in lined spiral notebooks. Each student was responsible for the notes and maps on the section of the site he excavated and each had his own notebook. This made writing this report after analysis in the laboratory a difficult task because of the complexity of correlating different students' notes. Nevertheless, it seems the best method to teach recording by making each student responsible for notes.

The following pages of the report are a descriptive explanation of the results of the excavation of six sites. The information, especially the architectural data, is presented in a telegraphic fashion and in a set format rather than in a narrative style. Only cardinal directions are used in description so that, for example, a wall which may be actually the northeast portion of the structure is designated as the north wall.

Ariz. D:11:3

Introduction

Ariz. D:11:3, a late Pueblo II-early Pueblo III site, is located on the east side of a gentle rise in the southeastern section of the Purple Sage Plateau Strip Mine area (J-3) (Fig. 12). It is approximately 1½ miles west of the main branch of Upper Moenkopi Wash, at an elevation of 6450 feet. A three-forked stick hogan and sweathouse complex, Ariz. D:11:4, is situated about 95 meters to the

FIGURE 12. *Oblique aerial view of Ariz. D:11:3 looking west.*

east of this site. The settlement consists of three contiguous masonry rooms and a connected jacal structure, an isolated subsurface mealing room, an isolated storage room, a kiva, and a large trash zone (Fig. 13).

Geologically, the site is on a layer of alluvium overlying bedrock (Mesa Verde sandstone). The sandstone outcrops near the top of the rise to the east and the floor of the three-room surface masonry structure is partially constructed upon bedrock. The alluvium layer becomes thicker and deeper further from the crest of the rise. The alluvium is a well sorted brown-tan sand and clay which is poorly consolidated. There is no obvious erosion at Ariz. D:11:3.

A small, deeply entrenched arroyo, approximately 100 meters to the east, drains the immediate area, and is part of the major Upper Moenkopi drainage system. The arroyo flows only seasonally, following heavy summer thunder shower activity and possibly after a rapid snowthaw.

Flora and fauna are typical of the Upper Sonoran ecological zone. On the slopes of this ridge are scattered piñon and juniper trees. The slope and flat on which the site is situated is covered with dead sagebrush, cholla, and delimiting the trash mound area, squawberry. The grasses present are blue grama, sand dropseed, and Indian rice grass.

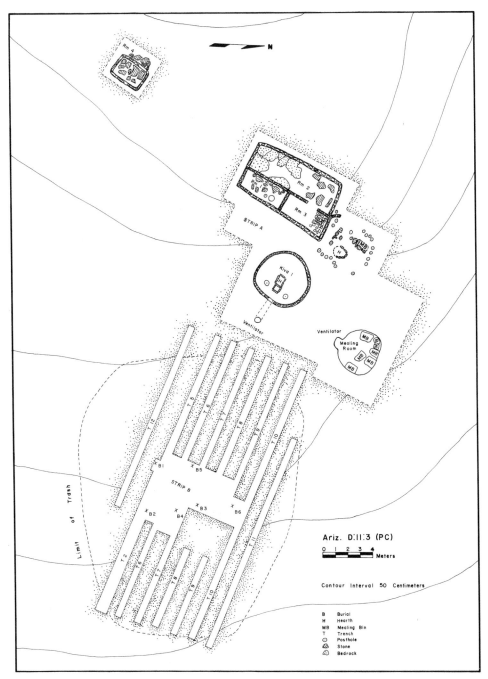

FIGURE 13. *Ariz. D:11:3. Plan view.*

Fauna was sparse. Various lizards, a prairie rattlesnake, and two cottontail rabbits were observed during excavation.

All the structures at the site were visible on the surface prior to excavation, except Mealing Room 1 and Room 5. The settlement was indicated by the rubble mounding of the major room-block Rooms 1, 2 and 3. Room 4, an isolated masonry storage unit, was plainly visible, and a slight depression between the room block and trash midden suggested the presence of the kiva. The trash midden was the most prominent feature at the site because of the extremely dark color of the soil and the dominance of *Lycium pallidum* on this highly organic disturbed soil. In fact, the concentration of *Lycium* on the trash mound made the site clearly visible during the helicopter survey.

Excavation began with test trenching for the kiva. As soon as the perimeter of the kiva was delimited, the fill, except for a stratigraphic block, was removed by hand shovel. Mealing Room 1 was detected by the north end of the exploratory trench which was excavated in the search for the walls of the kiva. The walls of the room block and storage unit were easily found by test trenches and the fill removed.

A one-meter square grid system was established over the midden although only portions of the midden were dug stratigraphically. When burials were encountered in the trash, the grid system was expanded when necessary. The fill from all one meter square grids which were excavated stratigraphically was sifted through quarter-inch mesh screen.

Ariz. D:11:3 was excavated because of its imminent destruction by coal mining operations and because it was the largest early Pueblo III site recorded at the time of excavation.

Architecture

Room 1 (Fig. 14, 15)

Type of Structure: Rectangular surface dwelling.

Dimensions: East-West, 1.7 m.; North-South, 3.8 m. Floor on old occupation surface.

Walls: Coursed tabular sandstone masonry with little intentional shaping. Minimum use of brown clay mortar. No evidence of plaster. Portions of east wall missing entirely. Maximum remaining height 50 cm., width 30 cm. Walls vary between one and two stones in width.

Entrance: Probably through roof.

Floor: Several large sandstone slabs near center. Maximum extension of sandstone slabs surface 2.2 m. Remainder of floor is hard packed, but unprepared native soil.

Hearth: Circular, 35 cm. diameter. Dish-shaped in cross section. Near northeast wall, unlined, but floor and walls burned to dark red color. No ash in fill.

Roof: Probably beams laid across uppermost course of masonry.

Fill: Brown aeolian sand with some small charcoal pieces. Numerous sand-

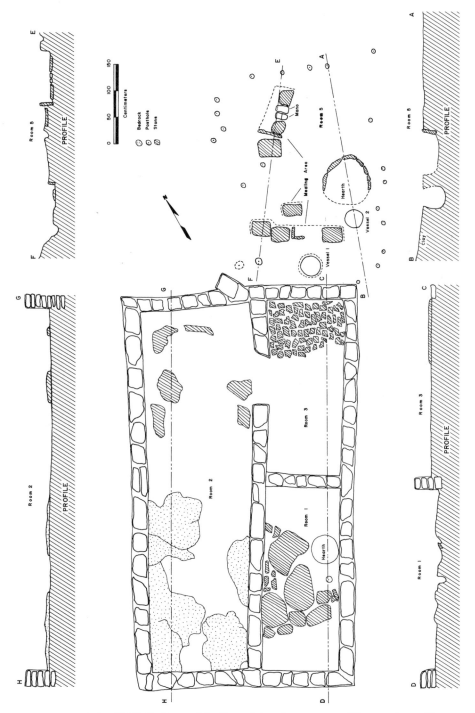

FIGURE 14. *Ariz. D:11:3. Room block and jacal structure. Plan and profile.*

[37]

FIGURE 15. *Ariz. D:11:3. Room block. View to north.*

stone pieces from upper courses of wall. No discernable difference between fill and floor fill.

Material Culture: Four two-hand manos in the fill.

Room 2 (Fig. 14)

Type of Structure: Rectangular storage unit (?).

Dimensions: East-West, 2.8 m.; North-South, 7.2 m. Floor on old occupation surface.

Walls: Masonry walls varying from two to five courses in height. Large tabular sandstone slabs. Cross wall on eastern portion of room composed of

[38]

FIGURE 16. *Ariz. D:11:3. Room 4. Slab-lined outlying storage room.*

thinner, more uniformly shaped sandstone slabs. Cross wall abuts exterior walls. Little use of brown clay mortar. No plaster. Average thickness of interior wall 30 cm. Portions of western section of wall missing.

Entrance: Probably through roof.

Floor: Unmodified sandstone bedrock composes much of southern portion. Rest of floor hard packed, native soil. Several unshaped sandstone slabs pave floor in north portion of room.

Roof: Probably beams laid across uppermost course of masonry.

Fill: Brown aeolian sand with some charcoal pieces. Not much sandstone rubble. Homogeneous throughout column.

Material Culture: Partially restorable corrugated vessel and Dogoszhi Black-on-white jar in fill.

Room 3 (Fig. 14)

Type of Structure: Rectangular surface dwelling.

Dimensions: East-West, 1.55 m.; North-South, 3.7 m. Floor on old occupation surface.

Walls: Coursed sandstone masonry of poor workmanship. Individual pieces minimally shaped. Small amounts of brown mud mortar. All of east and north wall collapsed. Portion of west wall missing. Average thickness 20 cm. Courses one to three stories wide. Maximum remaining height 57 cm.

Entrance: Probably through roof.

Floor: Small, fiitted sandstone chunks pave 120 cm. of north portion. Hard packed native soil forms remainder of floor. No plaster noted. Unpaved portion in poor condition.

Hearth: Circular, 48 cm. in diameter; 38 cm. deep. Unlined. Bowl-shaped in cross section. Brown sand walls baked red. No ash in fill.

Roof: Probably beams laid across uppermost course of wall.

Fill: Tan-brown between large amounts of fallen masonry. Most fallen masonry in upper sections of fill. Floor fill not distinguishable from fill.

Material Culture: Two worked sherds in fill.

Room 4 (Fig. 16)

Type of Structure: Rectangular surface storage unit.

Dimensions: East-West, 1.5 m.; North-South, 2.6 m. Floor on old occupation surface.

Walls: Large sandstone slabs set vertically into old occupation surface. Small pieces used for chinking. No mortar or plaster remains between slabs. Maximum height of walls 53 cm. Portions of east wall collapsed.

Entrance: Probably through roof.

Floor: Large fitted sandstone slabs with some stone chinking. Brown clay plaster fills interstices between slabs.

Roof: Possibly beams laid across top of upright slabs and additional slabs laid over beams forming a rodent-proof storage room. Large slabs in upper portions of fill probably are roofing slabs.

Fill: Rubble from the roof and upper walls, and brown sand flecked with charcoal.

Material Culture: One trough and one fragmentary metate in fill.

Room 5 (Fig. 14, 17)

Type of Structure: Rectangular jacal dwelling.

Dimensions: East-West, 3.05 m.; North-South, 4 m. Depth of floor varies from old occupation surface at north end to 53 cm. below surface at south end.

Walls: North, east and west walls jacal; south wall masonry. Jacal walls now represented by fragmentary juniper posts burned off at ground level. Posts in east wall were placed close together in a trench suggesting a jacal structure rather than a summer shade. South wall a maximum of five courses high at present and 41 cm. in height; relatively long well-shaped sandstone blocks. Abundant use of brown clay mortar. No plaster. No prepared footing. Each course one stone wide. Southwest masonry corner curves slightly to meet jacal wall.

Entrance: Although no definite entry is distinguishable, it is assumed that if the entry is in the wall it is along the west wall or near the northeast corner since these areas have the widest spaced postholes. The fact that the structure is jacal, however, does not preclude the possibility of a roof entry.

FIGURE 17. *Ariz. D:11:3. Room 5. A jacal structure contiguous with the masonry room block. Stakes indicate postholes.*

Floor: Red-brown native soil hard packed from use. No special preparation noted. Northward slope of the natural surface necessitated some excavation to ensure a level floor. Consequently, the southern portion of the floor was excavated 53 cm. below the old occupation surface. Floor slopes up gradually at south side to meet masonry wall. Two cracked Tusayan Corrugated jars which probably served as permanent storage containers were plastered into the floor in the southeast quadrant of the room.

Hearth: Circular, 70 cm. diameter, 39 cm. deep. Slab-lined on sides with clay mortar between slabs and on bottom of hearth. Light gray wood ash in fill to floor level.

Mealing Bins: Nine mealing bins are grouped into three areas. One series of four contiguous bins oriented north-south and located near the northwest corner. Grinding was done toward the east. Four contiguous bins are located near the center of the south wall and oriented east-west. Grinding was toward the north.

The ninth mealing bin is situated 35 cm. north of the bins described above. Grinding was toward the east. Only one of the bins has remaining upright slabs. The other bins are characterized by a flat slab plastered into the floor at the base of the bin and by the sloping walls dug into the floor. No metates were remaining in any bins.

Roof: The roof was preserved by burning and collapsed onto the floor. Hori-

[41]

FIGURE 18. *Ariz. D:11:3. Mealing Room 1. View is to the south.*

zontal juniper beams were covered at right angles by juniper shakes. Brush and grass were placed over the shakes and a 3 to 5 in. covering of mud formed the top covering. Mud coating burned red from fire.

Fill: Brown loosely consolidated sand with small amounts of charcoal. Little sandstone rubble. Fill easily distinguishable from floor fill because of collapsed roof.

Material Culture: Eight two-hand manos and one one-hand mano plus a hammerstone, miniature pottery burden basket, and fragmentary red siltstone disk in fill; metate fragment and two two-hand manos in floor fill.

Mealing Room 1 (Fig. 18, 19)

Type of Structure: Subsurface oval mealing room with southern ventilator shaft.

Dimensions: East-West, 3.3 m.; North-South, 3.6 m. Average depth of floor 1.43 m. below present ground surface.

Walls: Formed by native soil into which structure was excavated. No plaster noted. Upper portions of walls eroded after abandonment of structure. Walls

FIGURE 19. *Ariz. D:11:3. Mealing Room 1. Details of mealing bins. Note rocks to support metate and to catch meal in the basins.*

uneven and slope inward toward floor. Postholes at old occupation surface suggest superstructure of perishable material.

Entrance: Probably through roof.

Floor: Naturally occurring gray clay directly overlying bedrock. Very uneven. Slight rise forming low bench along north wall. No special preparation noted.

Hearth: Length 39 cm., width 30 cm., depth 23 cm. Unprepared burned gray clay. Rounded rectangle in shape. Basin shaped in cross section. Brown sand and clay in fill.

Mealing Bins: Seven mealing bins are grouped in three areas. One series of four contiguous mealing bins oriented east-west located near the north wall. Grinding was done toward the north. Two contiguous mealing bins oriented north-south are located against the east wall. Grinding was toward a central area between the opposing bins. The seventh mealing bin is against the west wall. Grinding was done toward the north. None of the bins were delineated by upright slabs. All were excavated into the floor and all but one have a slab set into the floor. Three bins have unshaped sandstone rocks in place to prop up a metate. No metates left in bins.

FIGURE 20. *Ariz. D:11:3. Kiva 1.*

Roof: Roof and upper walls of perishable material. Three postholes at old occupation surface around perimeter of structure suggest upper walls slant inward to form roof. Several horizontal juniper beams in upper portions of fill probably from roof on upper portions of wall.

Fill: Well-consolidated tan-brown sand with little charcoal flecking. Fill difficult to distinguish from undisturbed soil. Fill consistent throughout column. No discernable difference between fill and floor fill.

Ventilator: In south wall. Masonry lined in part on vertical back wall and vertical collapsed masonry facing wall above ventilator opening. Ventilator was probably formed by excavating a deep niche into the wall and then constructing a masonry facing. Ventilator opening probably rectangular, 60 cm. wide. Vent floor 43 cm. above floor of structure.

Material Culture: Fifteen hammerstones, a pecking stone, grinding slab, and three two-hand manos in fill. One sherd spindle whorl, seven two-hand manos, and two metate fragments in fill; three two-hand manos, a metate fragment, a small milling stone, two waste flakes, a siltstone pendant and a pecking stone in floor fill.

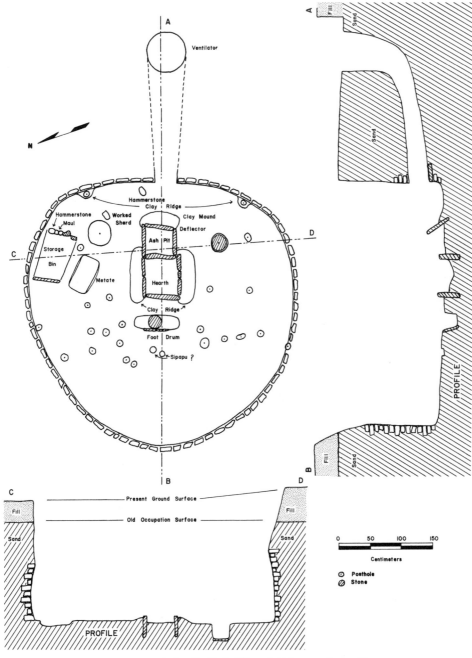

FIGURE 21. *Ariz. D:11:3. Kiva 1. Plan and profile.*

Kiva 1 (Fig. 20, 21)
   Type of Structure: Slightly "D" shaped; subsurface ceremonial room.

Dimensions: East-West, 4.2 m.; North-South, 4.2 m.; average depth of floor from present ground surface, 2.0 m.; from old occupation surface, 1.6 m.

Walls: Coursed sandstone masonry of much finer quality than surface masonry rooms. Individual pieces are small, well-fitted and thin. Minimum use of brown clay mortar. An occasional sherd used for chinking. Three gaps in masonry to accommodate roof support posts. Masonry remains to maximum of 1.35 m. above floor. Upper courses of masonry collapsed into fill. South portion of wall tilting inward probably after abandonment. Three coats of thin brown clay plaster extending presently a maximum of 27 cm. above floor. Surface of each clay layer slightly smoke blackened.

Entrance: Probably through opening in roof.

Floor: Brown-gray clay plaster with numerous charcoal particles. Good condition. Rounds up slightly to walls.

Postholes: Twenty small holes, averaging 6 cm. in diameter, found mainly in west portion of floor. All filled with fine, red-brown sand. Many may not have held posts. Two primary postholes in east half of floor; north posthole 35 cm. in diameter and 34 cm. in depth with prepared clay floor; south posthole 30 cm. in diameter and 20 cm. in depth with inverted stone slab pallet for base. Three small posts plastered behind walls at a gap in masonry. Small posts probably secondary roof support posts.

Hearth: Rectangular slab-lined with clay bottom. Depth 48 cm., length 60 cm., width 55 cm. Light gray wood ash in fill to top of slab lining. Clay rimmed around slabs on north and south sides.

Ashpit: East of and adjoining hearth. Rectangular slab-lined with clay bottom. Length 49 cm., maximum width 48 cm., depth 39 cm. Small charcoal particles and brown sand in fill.

Deflector: Sandstone slab forming west wall of ashpit. Length 59 cm., maximum thickness 2.5 cm. Top broken off. Clay rimmed around east side.

Storage Bin: Near northeast wall. Length 70 cm., width 40 cm., depth 5-10 cm. Slab-lined on west wall. Remainder plastered like floor. Fill similar to floor fill.

Foot Drum: Sub-rectangular, unlined. West of hearth 23 cm. Length 73 cm., width 15 cm. Circular stone disk at floor opening. V-shaped in cross section.

Roof: Probably quadrilateral arrangement of roof supports suggests a rectangular plate on which horizontal timbers were placed. Sides probably formed by small poles presenting appearance of truncated pyramid. No major roof support postholes in east section of floor makes roof shape determination problematical.

Fill: Nine distinct stratigraphic zones in fill and floor fill (Fig. 22). All zones natural except for burned roofing material 5-10 cm. above floor. Four major layers of aeolian and alluvial derived sand and clay interspersed with thin charcoal layers. No trash filled zones. Floor fill below burned roofing material indistinguishable from fill directly above fallen roof. Numerous sandstone construction blocks throughout column presumably from masonry surface rooms.

FIGURE 22. *Ariz. D:11:3. Kiva 1. Stratigraphic column with numerous water and wind laid laminae.*

Ventilator: Square opening, 30 cm. wide, in center of west wall 23 cm. above floor. Slab-lined on bottom to 25 cm. behind opening. Vertical length of tunnel 2.05 m. Diameter of opening at surface 50 cm.

Material Culture: Four two-hand manos, one one-hand mano, one miniature pottery burden basket, two waste flakes, a polishing stone, and a bone awl in fill; two two-hand manos, two utilized flakes, a worked sherd and a pecking and polishing stone in floor fill; one two-hand mano, two metates, a maul, hammerstone, and a worked sherd on floor.

Architectural Summary

The village pattern at Ariz. D:11:3 is typical of the late Pueblo II-early Pueblo III orientation. Upslope and furthest west is the room block containing both masonry and jacal structures. Immediately to the east is a single kiva. North of the kiva and northeast of the room block is a semi-subterranean mealing room. Excavations at other sites indicate that this is a characteristic location of semi-subterranean mealing rooms. The small storage room is located south of the room block. The large trash midden is east of the kiva.

There is no indication of differing construction periods. All structures appear to have been built at the same time. All dividing walls in the room block abut the exterior walls rather than being bonded in the exterior walls. In addition, there is no indication of any structure being abandoned before the rest of the site. The fill, in all structures, is natural rather than trash filled. Both the kiva and Room 5 (the jacal structure) had burned, apparently when the site was abandoned.

The poor quality of construction is typical of the Kayenta Anasazi. There is a minimum of shaping of sandstone; consequently, walls are uneven and the individual stones fit poorly. An exception is the kiva, which was constructed of smaller, better shaped sandstone pieces and plastered over. The semi-subterranean mealing structure was unlined, neither plaster nor masonry being used.

Refuse

The refuse midden was gridded into one meter squares and, in part, the midden was excavated in this grid system in 15 cm. levels.

The trash, represented by charcoal and ash stained sand, sherds, and utilized and unutilized stone, was slightly mounded with a maximum depth near the center of one meter. The trashy soil was extremely dark from the high organic content and yet screening and close inspection of the soil revealed virtually no floral, and few faunal, remains. The trash zone was extremely disturbed by rodent activity causing considerable mixture and disturbance of burials located in and below the refuse. Profiles of the trash area and seriation of types were attempted but no pattern of stylistic change was observed. This may indicate a short temporal span or a complete mixing of trash by rodent and root actions.

Other Excavations

A backhoe was used to dig fourteen test trenches north and south of the structures in an unsuccessful attempt to locate subsurface rooms.

Artifacts

Chipped Stone Artifacts

Chipped stone, both in the form of tools and debitage, is rare at Ariz. D:11:3. In spite of the great amount of screening of trash, only a handful of chipped stone was recovered. The scarcity of chipped stone is a function of the absence of any fine grain pebbles suitable for chipping on Black Mesa. The Mesa Verde sand-

FIGURE 23. *Chipped stone artifacts from various sites. A, concave scraper; B, side scraper; C, knife; D, projectile point; E, drill.*

stone, which forms Black Mesa, contains no quartz or chert pebbles and consequently all chipped stone had to be obtained from a considerable distance.

One well made white chert *knife* (Fig. 23) was found in the trash midden. The triangular blade has a straight base and is bifacially flecked. Secondary chipping is bifacial. The base is slightly convex. The length of the blade is 6 cm.; the width at the base is 2.5 cm. One jasper drill was excavated at the site. It is 2.5 cm. in length, 0.4 cm. in width, with a thickness of 0.3 cm. The drill is constructed from one long narrow flake which is triangular in cross section. Two of the edges have been sharpened by unifacial chipping; the tip is blunt. The proximal surface is the cortex of the pebble from which the drill was fashioned.

Four sub-rectangular *side scrapers* were found at Ariz. D:11:3. Three are chert and one quartzite; no cortex remains on any of the scrapers. Secondary chipping along two edges is present on one scraper; the others are unifacially worked. Lengths range from 2.9 cm. to 6.4 cm., widths from 2.1 cm. to 4.0 cm. Ten *utilized* chert *flakes* were found at the site, nine in the trash mound and one in the floor fill of Kiva 1. Use scars are indicated along one edge of eight of the flakes. Two flakes have two utilized edges. No cortex is remaining on seven of the

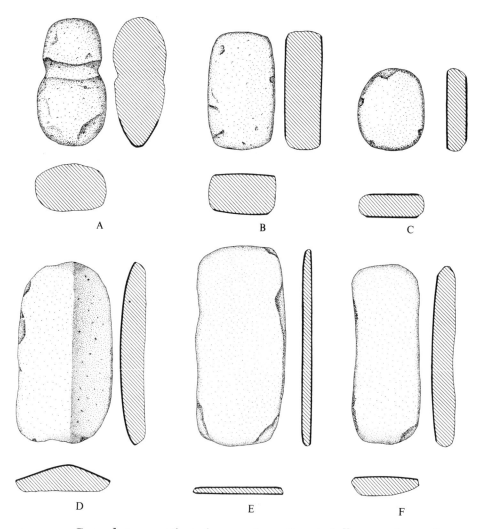

FIGURE 24. *Ground stone artifacts from various sites. A, full-grooved axe; B, one hand sub-rectangular mano; C, one hand oval mano; D, two hand faceted mano, convex use surface; E, two hand mano, flat use surfaces; F, two hand mano, convex use surface. Length of F, 23.6 cm.*

flakes. The flakes range in length from 2.0 cm. to 6.3 cm., in width from 1.0 cm. to 4.2 cm. and 0.5 cm. to 1.5 cm. in thickness. Fifteen *waste flakes* of calcedony, chert, and quartzite were excavated from the site. No evidence of usage is present on the flakes.

Ground Stone Artifacts

Ground stone tools are relatively plentiful. The majority of the items are manos and metates, indicating an emphasis on the grinding of plant products. All ground stone is Mesa Verde sandstone. The majority of the artifacts are well-

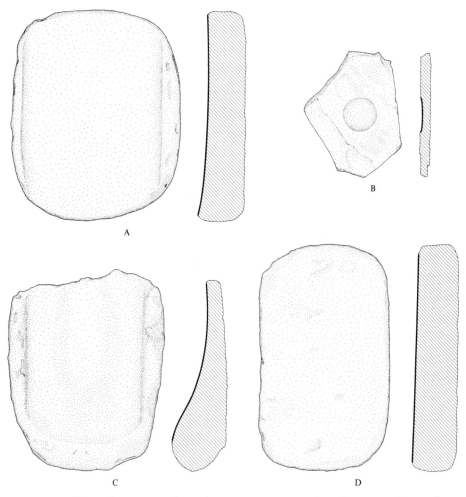

FIGURE 25. *Ground stone artifacts from various sites. A, full-grooved trough metate; B, palette; C, trough metate, open on one end; D, flat metate. Length of A, 49 cm.*

worn or broken. Few of the manos and metates show only little wear suggesting that only old and discarded tools were left behind when the site was abandoned.

One hundred and six partial and whole two-hand *manos* (Fig. 24) were excavated, ranging in length from 3.6 cm. to 30 cm. and in width from 3.4 cm. to 14 cm. All the manos are of fine to medium grain sandstone. Ninety-six of the manos are unifacially ground; ten have two use surfaces. Two parallel use surface manos are present; of the remainder, seventy-eight have convex grinding surfaces, nine are flat and thirty are faceted. All the manos are sub-rectangular in shape; the edges chipped, then partially ground to shape. Six manos show evi-

[51]

dence of fire blackening; two have red pigment stains on one surface. One mano has an abrading groove at one end of the ventral surface. A mano blank, with edges chipped and shaped, and the ventral surface slightly smoothed, is present. Only ten of the manos are whole. Almost all are extremely worn.

Eight manos are of the one-hand variety, ranging in length from 5.6 cm. to 13 cm. and in width from 6.3 cm. to 10.4 cm. Four of the manos are rectangular in shape. The remainder are ovoid. All the manos are of fine to medium grain sandstone; four are unifacially ground and four are bifacially ground. The rectangular manos have convex grinding surfaces and were utilized in a reciprocal grinding fashion. Three of the ovoid manos are smoothed and ground on two surfaces; one is only slightly ground on one surface.

TABLE 5. *Mano types from Ariz. D:11:3.*

One-Hand Mano	8	Two-Hand Mano	106
Unifacial	5	Unifacial	96
Bifacial	3	Bifacial	10
Surface Convex	8	Faceted	30
Surface Flat		Surface Convex	78
		Surface Flat	9
		Total	114

Ten whole and fragmentary *metates* were recovered. Two of the metates, one fragmentary and one whole, are of the full-trough variety. Both are made of fine grain sandstone, with edges chipped then partially ground to shape. The whole metate measures 48 cm. in length and 30 cm. in width; the fragmentary metate is 33 cm. in length with a width of 22 cm. One flat metate, sub-rectangular in shape and made from fine grain sandstone, has a smoothly pecked use surface. The dorsal surface and edges are roughly worked to shape; the maximum length is 51 cm. and the width is 30.8 cm. A fine grain sandstone trough metate, open at one end, has two ground surfaces on its ventral side. The main trough is 25 cm. in width; a second, narrower trough, 15 cm. wide, is ground through the center of the first. The length of the metate is 45.5 cm., with a fragment missing at the open end; width is 35 cm. The remaining six metates are fragmentary, ranging in length from 6.9 cm. to 40 cm. and width from 9.6 cm. to 25 cm. All are made from fine to coarse grain sandstone. The fragments show evidence of a trough with edges chipped and ground.

A slightly troughed sandstone *grinding slab* was located in Mealing Room 1. Its length is 22.9 cm., and the width is 16 cm. The use surface of the slab is uneven with a slight ground depression in the trough at the thicker end. There is a slight ridge along one side of the trough. One fine grain sandstone *abrading stone* was excavated from Kiva 1. It is sub-rectangular in shape. The use surface is ground smooth, all other faces are unworked. Its length is 11.0 cm. and the width is 10.2 cm.

[52]

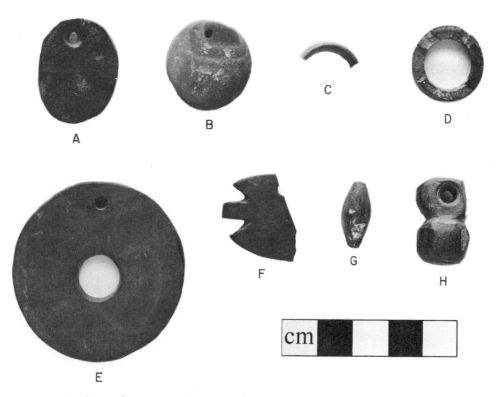

FIGURE 26. *Ground stone artifacts of adornment from various sites. A, B, sandstone pendants; C, D, finger rings; E, F, siltstone pendants; G, H, sandstone ornaments.*

A *milling stone*, located in the floor fill of Mealing Room 1, is made from a roughly pentagonal shaped piece of tan sandstone, 29 cm. in length and 23 cm. in width. A ground circular depression, 12 cm. in diameter, is situated in the center of the ventral side of the stone. The ventral surface is slightly ground, and the dorsal surface is unworked. A small chip is missing from one portion of the edge of the depression. A thin hexagonal *palette* (Fig. 23) constructed of fine grain sandstone was found inverted at the bottom of a major roof support posthole in Kiva 1; its length is 28 cm. and the maximum width is 25 cm. A small, circular depression, 8.2 cm. in diameter, is ground in the center of the ventral surface. The depth of the depression is 0.5 cm. The surface of the depression is stained red from grinding pigment.

One fine grain sandstone *pestle* was found in the trash midden. Its shape is cylindrical, tapering toward the proximal end; the length is 7.5 cm. and width is 5.3 cm. The proximal end shows pounding and pecking scars; the distal end, which is rounded and is smooth, shows no evidence of pounding. The body of the pestle is ground smooth, with some small areas of pitting present. One coarse

[53]

grain, fully grooved sandstone *maul* was found; its length is 15.3 cm., the width, 9.4 cm. The maul is ovoid in cross section, with a slight ridge present on each side of the hafting groove. The poll is rounded, with the ventral surface pecked. The bit is dulled with pounding scars. One side is partially flattened by grinding.

One whole and three fragmentary stone *finger rings* (Fig. 26) were recovered. Two are dark grey, extremely fine grain sandstone; the remaining are fine grain shale stone, opaque white and reddish brown. The fragments are polished; striations are present on the exterior and interior portions of the ring. They range in length from 1.4 cm. to 1.6 cm. and in width from 1 cm. to 1.3 cm. The whole ring is 2 cm. in diameter. The highly polished ring is complete in its circumference, but three-quarters of the width is broken off. The edge is ground, and on the fragmented side, rough and chipped. Maximum width is 0.6 cm. and the minimum width is 0.3 cm.

Eight small, ground *pendants,* whole and partial, were excavated from varied proveniences. They range in diameter from 2.2 cm. to 5.8 cm. Six are made of red siltstone; the remaining two, mudstone and quartzite. One is whole with two biconical holes, one near the center, and the other near the edge. Three others have biconical holes, two near the edge, and one in the center. All are ground smooth on both faces, with ground edges. Presumably they were suspended and used for decoration.

Eleven miscellaneous pieces of ground sandstone, ranging from fine to coarse grain, were found at the site. Their function is indeterminate. Four of the pieces are ground on two sides; three are convex on the ventral surface, one is concave. Two pieces show grinding on only one side; the dorsal surface of one is ground smooth with a diagonal groove present. The seventh piece of sandstone is ground smooth on the ventral surface and is covered with a yellow pigment. The ventral surface of the eighth piece is circular with a concave central depression; the dorsal surface is slightly concave. The remaining pieces are fragmentary and may be portions of manos or metates.

Two stone *beads* were located at the site. The first is one-half of a polished quartzite bead. A conical hole is ground through the center with a diameter of 0.7 cm.; total diameter is 1.6 cm., with a thickness of 0.6 cm. The second is a small, white stone bead with a diameter of 0.3 cm. and width of 0.1 cm.

One irregularly shaped piece of worked, red siltstone was found. Two edges are ground smooth, with one end rounded. The length is 2.1 cm. and width is 1.7 cm.

Twenty-three *hammerstones* were found at the site. Nineteen are quartzite, one is chert, and three are petrified wood. All the hammerstones are unshaped and the majority are ovoid to trapezoidal in form; one hammerstone is missing two large flakes, with poundscars along the flake ridges. All show evidence of battering along one or more surfaces. Lengths range from 3 cm. to 11.3 cm., with widths from 2 cm. to 9.6 cm.

Three smooth, unmodified pebbles utilized as *pecking stones* were excavated at the site. All are gray-black quartz and ovoid. Two of the stones show evidence of battering and pecking at both ends; each is pecked on one side. The third stone is flat, one end fragmented from use. The undamaged end is pecked in one area. Slight pitting occurs on both surfaces of the stone. Length ranges from 4.5 cm. to 5.2 cm., the width from 3.5 cm. to 4.5 cm. These pecking stones probably served the function of small hammerstones. Three unmodified, highly smoothed pebbles, often referred to as *polishing stones,* were excavated at the site. One exhibits a high degree of luster on all faces. Two of the stones are quartzite; one is of chalcedony. One stone is fractured at one end. The function of the stones is unknown, since the high luster may have been imparted by natural agencies. They are not indigenous to the area. The stones vary in length from 3.3 cm. to 5.2 cm., and in width from 2.5 cm. to 5 cm.

One thick, circular, fine grain sandstone *disc* was located in the foot drum at floor level in Kiva 1. The function is unknown. The diameter of the stone is 23 cm.; the thickness is 8 cm. Some pecking was done to smooth the ventral surface. The dorsal surface is slightly concave; the central portion is a lighter color than the periphery edges. The sides and edges are slightly rounded and ground smooth.

Twelve pieces of *pigment* were recovered from Ariz. D:11:3. Two are irregularly shaped limonite, from Mealing Room 1 and Room 5. Of the four pieces of red pigment, one piece is partially ground along one edge; the remaining pieces are unworked. The remaining irregularly shaped pieces are yellow, possibly ochre. One piece is worked, three have rounded edges and the last two are unmodified.

Ceramics

Tusayan White Ware and Tusayan Gray Ware are predominant at Ariz. D:11:3. Sosi Black-on-white and Dogoszhi Black-on-white, with 1,608 and 1,422 sherds respectively, are the two most common types. Black Mesa Black-on-white is represented by 871 sherds. In the gray ware category, Tusayan Corrugated, with 11,503 sherds, is the dominant type. Tusayan Black-on-red with 947 sherds is the most prevalent Tsegi Orange Ware.

Twenty-one whole or partially restorable vessels were recovered from the site; of these, eight are classified as miniatures. The remaining standard size vessels are almost evenly divided in number between Tusayan White Ware and Tusayan Gray Ware.

One slipped Tusayan White Ware deep bowl without painted design was found in association with Burial 5 (Fig. 8, C). It has a U-shaped horizontal handle on one side. Scattered on the floor of Room 2 was a large, partially restorable Dogoszhi Black-on-white narrow-mouthed jar (Fig. 10, C). The neck design is wide lined, Sosi Black-on-white in appearance, with the body of the vessel decorated with a hatched curvilinear Dogoszhi design. A Dogoszhi Black-on-white pitcher, found with Burial 2, is whole except for two chips from the rim (Fig. 8, D). It has a broad, cross-hatched design around the neck, with the body of the pitcher covered by a broad, hatched design. The handle is attached from the rim

TABLE 6. *Provenience of pottery types from Ariz. D:11:3.*

Type	Surface	Strip A	Strip	Room 1 Fill	Room 2 Fill	Room 2 Floor	Room 3 Fill	Room 4 Fill
Tusayan White Ware	4	2	72	81	14	2	7	56
Kana-a B/W			2					
Black Mesa B/W	6	1	44	12	4	1		15
Sosi B/W	7		41	45	11	1	8	55
Dogoszhi B/W	12	2	33	22	4		1	19
Flagstaff B/W	3		2		1			
Shato Variety								
Unclassified B/W	1	2	34	24	10		4	10
Tusayan Gray Ware			44	9	1	2	7	3
Honani Tooled								
Tusayan Corrugated	5	7	290	113	27	30	15	95
Moenkopi Corrugated	1	3	13	20		4		4
Kiet Siel Gray								
Coconino Gray	1							
Tusayan Applique								
Tsegi Orange Ware	3		24	11	2			5
Medicine B/R			3					4
Tusayan B/R	11		40	13	1	1		11
Tusayan Polychrome	1			1				4
Tsegi R/O				1				
Deadmans B/R	1							
San Juan Red Ware	1							
Unclassified Orange								
Total	57	17	642	352	75	41	42	281

TABLE 6. *Provenience of pottery types from Ariz. D:11:3.*

Room 4 Floor Fill	Room 5 Fill	Room 5 Floor	Mealing Room 1 Fill	Mealing Room 1 Floor Fill	Mealing Room 1 Floor	Mealing Room 1 Sub-floor	Kiva 1 Fill	Kiva 1 Floor Fill	Kiva 1 Floor	Burial Fill	Combined Test Trenches	Totals
18	68	2	80	19	6	2	49	8	5	515	2,322	3,332
												2
4	10		22	1	2		10			136	592	860
20	92	5	44	4	3	5	53	17		230	954	1,595
4	30		44	4	2	13	53	4	1	180	987	1,415
	2							3		36	45	92
			1							5	21	27
	36		41	2	5	1	11	11	1	204	1,110	1,507
3	19	1	24	4	7	1	34	1	1	195	621	977
										2		2
36	225	2	316	34	16	3	290	50	3	1,842	8,114	11,513
9	33		73	3	2	1	90	17	8	90	297	668
			6								17	23
												1
											1	1
1	18		23	2	3		17			128	580	817
			1							19	80	107
7	11	1		4	6	1	13	2		207	618	947
1	4									7	11	29
											1	2
												1
												1
											6	6
103	548	11	675	77	52	27	620	113	19	3,796	16,377	23,925

TABLE 7. *Whole and restorable vessels from Ariz. D:11:3.*

Type	Form	Maximum Diameter	Rim Diameter	Volume	Height	Provenience	Figure
Black Mesa B/W	Bowl	6.8 cm.	6.8 cm.		4.5 cm.	Burial 2	8, F
Black Mesa B/W	Bowl	11.3 cm.	11.3 cm.	220 ml.	5.9 cm.	Burial 2	8, G
Black Mesa B/W	Jar	8.1 cm.	3.9 cm.	220 ml.	9.2 cm.	Burial 4	9, D
Black Mesa B/W	Jar					Burial 3	
Dogoszhi B/W	Jar	12.0 cm.	6.2 cm.	730 ml.	13.8 cm.	Burial 2	8, D
Dogoszhi B/W	Jar	41.0 cm.	15.0 cm.			Room 2	10, D
Sosi B/W	Bowl	22.5 cm.	22.5 cm.	2240 ml.	11.0 cm.	Burial 4	8, E
Sosi B/W	Bowl*					Kiva 1, Floor	
Unident. B/W	Jar	1.6 cm.	1.0 cm.	0.5 ml.	1.8 cm.	Test Trench 2	
Unident. B/W	Bowl	7.2 cm.	7.2 cm.	50.0 ml.	3.5 cm.	Exterior Pueblo Trench	
Unident. B/W	Bowl*	6.7 cm.	6.7 cm.		3.4 cm.	Burial 2	
Unident. B/W	Jar	7.2 cm.	4.2 cm.	160 ml.	8.6 cm.	Burial 5	
Unident. B/W	Jar	5.9 cm.			3.0 cm.	Test Trench 2	
Tsegi Orange	Bowl	23.5 cm.	23.5 cm.		14.0 cm.	Burial 4	
Tusayan B/R	Bowl	20.9 cm.	20.9 cm.		20.1 cm.	Burial 2	
Tusayan White Ware	Bowl	12.8 cm.	12.8 cm.	340 ml.	5.6 cm.	Burial 5	8, C
Kiet Siel Corrug.	Jar	14.9 cm.	13.1 cm.	1870 ml.	17.2 cm.	Burial 5	
Tusayan Corrug.	Jar					Burial 1	
Tusayan Corrug.	Jar	37.4 cm.				Room 5	10, A
Tusayan Corrug.	Jar	39.9 cm.				Room 5	10, B
Gray Ware	Jar	6.1 cm.	5.0 cm.		5.6 cm.	Burial 4	

*(frag.)

to the beginning of the curvature of the body. Two Sosi Black-on-white bowls, one whole and one represented by two pieces, were recovered from Burial 4 and Kiva 1, respectively. The fragmentary pieces have an exterior design of solid lines and triangles, with a scraped interior. The whole vessel is a deep bowl with an interior design of medium width black lines with scalloped-edged triangles (Fig. 8, E).

The remaining decorated ware vessels are both Black Mesa Black-on-white. One is a wide-mouthed jar found in association with Burial 3. The design consists of one exterior band of solid right triangles with a line radiating from the angle point; pendant dots are formed on one side of each line. A small, deep bowl was recovered from Burial 2. It has an interior design consisting of two panels of black and white diamonds, with a white strip separating the two panels.

Four utility vessels were recovered. Two Tusayan Corrugated storage vessels were discovered inserted into the floor of Room 5. Both are wide-mouthed jars and are fragmentary, though partially restored. One other Tusayan Corrugated was found in direct association with Burial 1. It is partially restored and seems to be a wide-mouthed jar. The remaining utility vessel is a Kiet Siel Corrugated jar found with Burial 5. It has a fire smudged exterior, with a handle attached from just under the rim to the beginning of the curvature of the body.

One Tsegi Orange Ware bowl, from Burial 4, shows the remnants of a black line design on the interior. It is fragmentary and the design is badly eroded. There is a red slip on the exterior. A partially restored Tusayan Black-on-red bowl was found with Burial 2. The interior design consists of three lines circling the rim, with lines radiating from the rim to the center of the bowl. There is a large fire cloud on the exterior.

All but one of the miniature vessels are Tusayan White Ware. The one gray ware vessel is fragmentary and was found with Burial 4. The bottom is flattened, though it is slightly convex on the interior. Two of the miniature vessels have Black Mesa Black-on-white design style. One is a fragmentary bowl, with a solid line and pendant dot design; while the other is a pitcher found with Burial 4. The neck design of the pitcher is of negative diamonds, with broad lines, and solid rectangles on the body. The remaining vessels are from assorted proveniences, and exhibit poorly executed designs. Three have faded and highly undefined patterns; two are bowls with interior decoration and one is a jar with an exterior design of random dots and lines. A miniature pitcher, from Burial 5, has a crudely executed design of solid triangles pendant from the rim. Opposing this, on the body of the pitcher, is a row of irregular black and white squares. The design is partially obscured by fire clouds. The final miniature vessel is a bowl, handle missing, with an interior design of wavy lines, solid triangles and interlocking hooks. There is a small fire cloud on the exterior.

Eleven worked sherds (Fig. 27), ten of Tusayan White Ware and one Tsegi Orange Ware, were excavated at the site. All but two are fragmentary. The orange ware sherd is scoop shaped with all edges ground. The length of the sherd is 7.6 cm., the maximum width, 6.3 cm. One white ware sherd is half-moon in shape. Both the concave and convex faces are covered with a white slip. The circular edge is ground; and the straight edge, fragmented. Its length is 4.1 cm. and the width is 2 cm. Two of the white ware sherds have no design element. One fragment is sub-rectangular, 7.3 cm. in length and 3 cm. in width. The other plain sherd is roughly rectangular, one edge rounded and ground. Its maximum length is 3.5 cm., the width, 2.8 cm. The seven remaining white ware sherds all have either a hatched or broadline design element present. Except for one circular sherd with a diameter of 2.5 cm., all are fragmentary with indications of cir-

FIGURE 27. *Worked black-on-white sherds from various sites.*

cular or sub-rectangular shapes. They range in length from 8.8 cm. to 1.1 cm., and in width from 7.1 cm. to 3.7 cm.

Several miscellaneous ceramic artifacts were found at the site. One partial Tusayan White Ware *spindle whorl*, 5.3 cm. in diameter, was found in Mealing Room 1. There is a biconical hole drilled through the center and a white slip on the concave side. One fragmentary white ware, lizard form applique 3 cm. long was found. Only the posterior end is present. Both feet are represented, but a portion of the tail is missing. It appears to have been affixed to the side of the vessel. The remaining three artifacts are of a type usually called *miniature burdenbaskets*. Two are black-on-red, one whole and one fragmentary. The latter is 1 cm. in length at the top of the basket and 0.7 cm. at the bottom. The former is 2.5 cm. in height and 2.2 cm. in length at the top. The remaining basket is gray ware and extremely crude. The basket length is 2.3 cm., the width is 1.3 cm.

Bone

Six bone *awls* (Fig. 28) were found at the site. Four are the splinter variety; two are the split-bone type. In the split-bone type, the head of the bone, in both cases, is ground, but the articular surfaces are relatively intact. One is stubby in

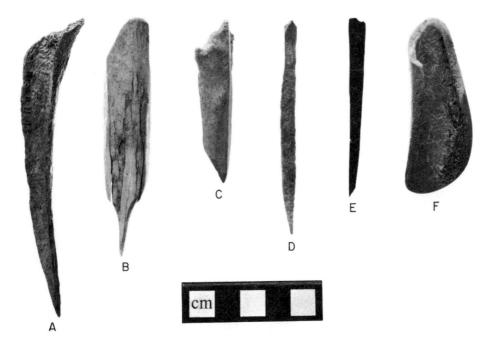

FIGURE 28. *Bone artifacts from various proveniences. A, B, C, D, E, bone awls; F, bone flesher.*

appearance with striations at the tip of the awl; the length is 4.9 cm. and the width of the base is 2 cm. There is a slight chip off of the tip; the awl is highly polished. The second awl, 6.3 cm. long and 1.6 cm. wide, has striations around the head; the tip end has ground edges and striations. Three of the remaining four are splinter awls; the fourth is an awl with the entire articular surface removed. The latter is burnt and the tip is broken off; the edges are ground and polished the full length of the awl. The butt end shows grinding near the proximal end. Its length is 6.9 cm.; the width of butt is 0.9 cm. The remaining three range in length from 4.6 cm. to 7.1 cm. and in width from 0.9 cm. to 1.3 cm. All are fragmentary; the edges are ground and striations are present near the tip ends. The exterior sides are polished with one interior grove worked and polished.

Shell

One olivella shell *bead* was excavated from the trash mound. The shell is whole and ground slightly at one end. A small chip is missing from the opposite end. Its length is 1.3 cm. and the median width is 0.6 cm.

Wood

A *Navajo wooden doll* (Fig. 29) was found on the surface between the kiva depression and the room block. The doll is roughly carved, and vaguely clothes-

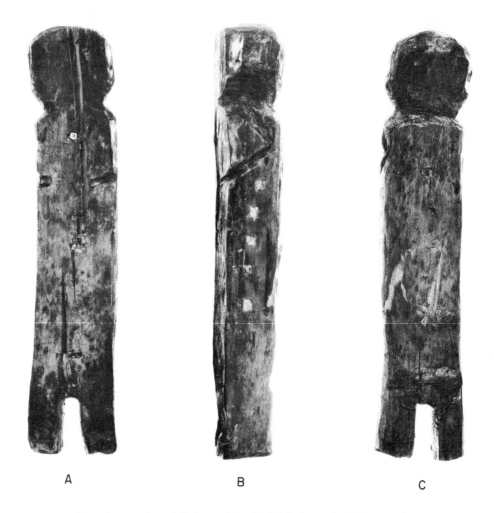

A   B   C

FIGURE 29. *Navajo wooden doll from Ariz. D:11:3. Length, 16.9 cm. A, front view; B, side view; C, back view.*

pin shaped. The head is suggested by two indentions on either side of the wood representing the neck. Arms and fingers are incised into the wood. No facial features are present. One white bead is located in the center of the chest. Along both sides are five square holes in a vertical line. Each square is filled with clay; one piece of chert or quartz is present in each square. A faded red outline, possibly indicative of clothing, is present on the front. Two oval holes, one filled with a red material, are located in the center of the back. Two incisions are present on the lower backside. The legs are short, with indentations indicating feet. Total

FIGURE 30. *Ariz. D:11:3. Burial 1. Note fragments of skull and large bones on sherd. Length of scale 5 cm.*

length of the doll is 16.9 cm. and the width is 3.7 cm. Two perforations are located on the bottom of the feet. One hole is on the top of the head.

Floral Materials

Three small charred corn cobs were found in fill around Burial 3. These specimens have been submitted to Dr. Hugh Cutler of the Missouri Botanical Garden for analysis.

Human Burials

Six human burials were recorded at Ariz. D:11:3. All burials were excavated from the refuse deposit to the east of the room block. During excavation it was apparent that some of the burials contained elements of other individuals. Osteological examinations revealed that there were parts of 14 individuals in what was recorded as six burials during excavation (Appendix I). It was necessary, however, to assign only a single burial number to closely associated groups of bones. This confusion is a result of the extremely disturbed condition of all individuals.

[63]

FIGURE 31. *Ariz. D:11:3. Burial 2. Note scattered remains of three individuals.*

All individuals, except Burial 5, were scattered apparently by rodents so that very few bones were still in an articulated position when excavated. Many of the long bones had been gnawed by rodents.

Burial 1 (Fig. 30)

This is the incomplete remains of a fetus of four to five lunar months. The skeletal remains were placed at a depth of 28 to 32 cm. from the present ground surface. The fetus was placed on the interior of a fragmentary Tusayan Corrugated jar. The orientation of the fetus was north to south with the skull probably to the south. No outline of a burial pit was observed and it is assumed that the sherd with the fetus was simply placed in a shallow hole directly in the trash zone. No funerary offerings were placed with the fetus.

Burial 2 (Fig. 31)

What is designated as Burial 2 is actually the scattered bones of three individuals. Because of the disturbed nature of the burial, it is impossible to say anything about orientation of the individual. No pit was noted and it appeared as if all the individual pieces of bone were disturbed. This is also indicated by the relatively great distance between different vessels placed with the burials. Individual bones were found from 14 to 37 cm. below the present ground surface. The following list of artifacts are all included as part of the burial offerings.

[64]

FIGURE 32. *Ariz. D:11:3. Burial 4. Burial in sitting position in pit. Skull is missing.*

Because of the disturbed nature of the burials and because of its position in the trash, some of these artifacts may not be associated with a burial. Five vessels were recovered: a miniature Black Mesa Black-on-white bowl, one black-on-white miniature bowl with badly faded black paint (the type of pottery is indeterminate), one small, deep Black Mesa Black-on-white bowl, one Dogoszhi Black-on-white pitcher, one Tusayan Black-on-red bowl, two worked sherds, one stone bead, and three pieces of yellow pigment and two pieces of red pigment.

Burial 3

This burial, containing elements of three individuals, is also in extremely poor condition. The bones range from 7 to 32 cm. below the present ground surface. No burial position could be determined, although the head may have been placed toward the south. The burial was not placed in a pit but was simply excavated into the trash zone above the sterile layer. In the fill, around the bones, were found one Black Mesa Black-on-white wide-mouthed jar, one worked sherd, one piece of red siltstone ground down at the edges and irregular in shape, one polished quartzite dark gray bead with a conical hole ground in the center, one stone awl, and two pieces of red pigment.

Burial 4 (Fig. 32)

This individual was placed in a pit dug into the sterile soil which lay below the trash zone. The pit is 70 cm. in diameter and is a maximum of 37 cm. below the bottom of the trash which is 45 to 50 cm. deep at this point in the refuse area. Many of the larger bones are articulated although the skull is missing, as are many of the smaller bones. The burial is placed in a seated position with the legs in the burial pit and the torso above the pit in the trash zone; the legs are loosely flexed with the knees underneath the trunk resting close together against the east wall of the burial pit. The back of the individual was positioned against the north edge of the pit. The vessels were placed near the pelvis to the west of the individual. Both arms are folded with the hands resting in the lap.

Burial 5 (Fig. 33)

Burial 5 is a four- or five-year-old child buried in a pit excavated in the sterile soil below the trash zone. The depth of the pit is 60 cm. below the bottom of the trash. The mouth of the pit is 45 cm. wide and 70 cm. long. The sides of the pit are slightly undercut. The opening was covered with a thin slab of Mesa Verde sandstone chipped to cover the mouth of the pit. The child was placed on the floor of the pit near the west wall on his right side. The legs are tightly flexed. The head is to the south. The arms are also in a flexed position with the hands pointing near the face. Three funerary vessels were placed on the floor of the cist east of the individual. A wide-mouthed Tusayan Corrugated jar was covered with a Tusayan White Ware bowl, which is undecorated. These vessels were placed near the center of the individual. Near the feet is a miniature black-on-white vessel. A small, partially ground piece of yellow ochre was found in the fill of the cist. The depth of the trash, above the slab covering of the cist, is 56 cm.

Burial 6

Burial 6 is actually various parts of three individuals. Virtually none of the

FIGURE 33. *Ariz. D:11:3. Burial 5. Top of pit was covered with large sandstone slab.*

bones are articulated. The bones, consisting mostly of ribs and long bones, were found in a massed area 18 to 24 cm. below the surface in the trash zone. No pit was observed and it is assumed that all elements have been disturbed to some extent. Because of the disturbed nature of the burial, no statements can be made concerning orientation of the individuals. No burial offerings were placed with the individuals.

Summary and Discussion

Ariz. D:11:3 is a Kayenta Anasazi habitation site consisting of three contiguous masonry rooms, one outlying masonry storage room, a jacal structure appended to the masonry room block, a kiva and a semi-subterranean mealing room. The permanence of the structures, and the large amount of trash without any visible stratigraphy, suggest a year around occupation over a fairly long period of time. The site may well have been occupied twenty-five or thirty-five years, if the amount of trash in relationship to the number of rooms is considered.

Ceramics, predominantly Sosi Black-on-white, Dogoszhi Black-on-white, and Tusayan Corrugated, suggest a late Pueblo II-early Pueblo III occupation and a date of about A.D. 1050–1150.

The large number of mealing bins, manos, and metates suggests the subsistence pattern centered around agriculture and collection of plants rather than hunting, even though floral remains are relatively scarce. The total lack of projectile points does not necessarily indicate a total lack of hunting with the bow and arrow, since the arrows may well have consisted solely of sharpened sticks with feather fletching as was found at Feather Cave (Ellis and Hammach 1968). The scarcity of fine grained chipping stones on the mesa is indicated in the absence of projectile points and the relative scarcity of chipped stone artifacts. What items were used for cutting and chiseling is not known.

There is little evidence of trade at Ariz. D:11:3. All ceramics are indigenous Kayenta Anasazi in spite of the fact that the excavated sherds were examined closely for possible Little Colorado White Ware and Mesa Verde White Ware. The only definite trade object is an olivella shell bead from the Gulf of Mexico found in the trash area. Chipped stone, both in the form of tools and debitage, is not indigenous to the region but may have been collected on trips to the Little Colorado or San Juan river areas rather than traded on to the mesa. All ground stone tools are manufactured from the indigenous Mesa Verde sandstone. Luxury goods are scarce, limited to a few finger rings and easily made siltstone pendants, suggesting a rather provincial and perhaps isolated settlement.

Architecturally, the site is quite varied, including poor quality masonry, jacal, masonry-lined subterranean structures, and unlined semi-subterranean structures.

A question arises concerning the relationship of Ariz. D:11:3 to surrounding sites in the immediate vicinity. Sites such as Ariz. D:11:2, Ariz. D:11:23, and Ariz. D:11:33 can be grouped, at least by ceramic evidence, in the same period as Ariz. D:11:3. In addition, there are numerous so-called "sherd areas" in the immediate drainage. Ariz. D:11:3 is by far the largest site, both in terms of visible structures and in the amount of trash. Consequently, the question arises: Is Ariz. D:11:3 more than simply a self-contained farming settlement, *i.e.*, did this settlement also serve for inter-settlement religious or economic participation for the nearby sites which have no masonry structures or no kiva? This is a question which cannot, as yet, be answered until more of the surrounding sites, especially the so-called sherd areas, are excavated. Furthermore, the ceramic evidence may be misleading; the fact that the ceramic assemblages are similar, indicating an occupation at a certain phase does not mean that the sites were exactly contemporaneous. The resolving element in this discussion of contemporaneity must await detailed analysis after excavation, the results of tree-ring analysis and archeomagnetic dating. Certainly, there is, as yet, not enough evidence to indicate exact contemporaneity nor to offer more than a suggestion that Ariz. D:11:3 may have had a key role in inter-settlement interaction. If, in addition, Ariz. D:11:3 was more than simply an independent habitation site, the absence of trade and luxury goods suggests the settlement could not have been much different than the

FIGURE 34. *Ariz. D:11:2. Oblique aerial view to the northeast.*

surrounding meaner sites. The presence of a kiva at this small site seems less unusual after even smaller sites were excavated which contain kivas.

Ariz. D:11:2

Introduction

Ariz. D:11:2 is located on the west edge of an east-west sandstone outcropping in the southeastern section of the J-3 strip mine area at an elevation of 6,470 feet (Fig. 34). The settlement is late Pueblo II-early Pueblo III and consists of three surface masonry rooms (Fig. 35). The site is approximately 1½ miles west of the main branch of the Upper Moenkopi Wash. To the north, south, and west of this habitation site are low alluvial-filled valleys which eventually drain into that wash. These low areas were undoubtedly utilized for agricultural activities. The soil cover over bedrock is sparse and, in many cases, the sandstone is outcropping. In Rooms 1 and 3 portions of the floor consist of bedrock. The soil cover is a sandy dark brown only partially held in place by scattered grasses and cacti. In the low, narrow alluvial valley to the southwest of the site, a headward-cutting arroyo is beginning to form.

The immediate environment of the site is designated as Upper Sonoran and is dominated by piñon and juniper on the upper slopes of the outcrop. There is some squawberry on the east side of the room block. Numerous species of lizards, scorpions and centipedes were noted during excavation and more than eight prairie rattlesnakes were killed during the excavations.

Prior to excavation, the site consisted of a readily apparent mound of masonry rubble in which at least one standing crosswall was visible. No kiva depression was noted. To the east of the room block on the slope, there is a scattering of sherds suggesting a slightly eroded trash area. The soil, in this region, is stained from organic material.

Ariz. D:11:2 was originally recorded from the air by Euler during his helicopter reconnaissance in 1967. The site was excavated because of its position within the strip mine area and because of its unusual environmental setting directly on the sandstone outcrop.

Architecture

Room 1 (Fig. 37)
　Type of Structure: Rectangular surface dwelling or storage unit.
　Dimensions: East-West, 1.7 m.; North-South, 4.9 m. Average depth of floor, 20 cm. above present ground surface. Fill was apparently used to level sections of the floor because of the bedrock base.
　Walls: Fine quality coursed masonry of well-shaped blocks rather than tabular sandstone pieces. Some small chinking between courses. Individual blocks have considerable modification by pecking and, in some cases, grinding. Small amounts of clay mortar used in west wall. No plaster noted. In some cases, wall footed directly on bedrock. Maximum remaining wall height: 82 cm. Average width: 35 cm. Walls in most cases one stone in width. Exterior walls abut southern cross wall.
　Entrance: Probably through roof.
　Floor: Light brown hard packed soil. Poor condition. No plastering noted. Portions of bedrock at floor level near south end. Floor-wall juncture at right angle. Fill probably put over bedrock to level floor since charcoal particles are present in places below floor. No floor features.
　Hearth: None.
　Roof: Several juniper tree-ring specimens collected 12 cm. above floor suggesting poles laid horizontally across upper course of wall.
　Fill: Light yellow-brown fine sand. Numerous sandstone blocks from fallen courses of wall in upper portions of fill. Fill homogeneous throughout column.
　Material Culture: Two hammerstones, one two-hand mano in fill. Two hammerstones and one waste flake in floor fill.

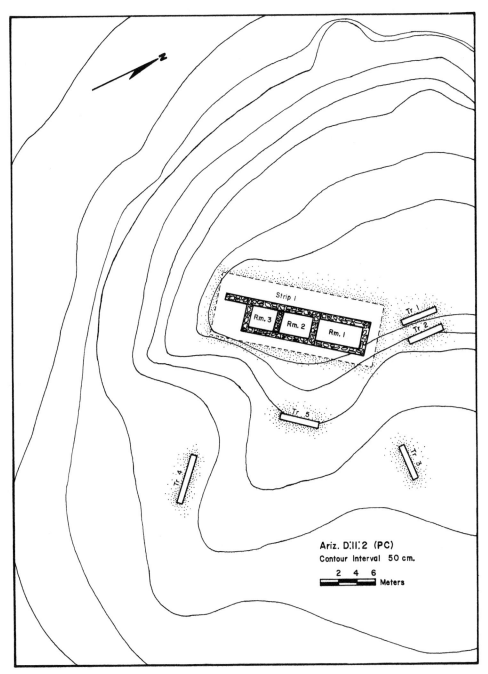

FIGURE 35. *Ariz. D:11:2. Plan view.*

FIGURE 36. *Ariz. D:11:2. Room block prior to excavation.*

FIGURE 37. *Ariz. D:11:2. Room block. View is to south.*

FIGURE 38. *Ariz. D:11:2. Cross wall of Room 2 constructed of small unshaped stones abutted by exterior wall.*

Room 2

> *Type of Structure:* Rectangular surface dwelling or storage room.
>
> *Dimensions:* East-West, 1.85 m.; North-South, 3.48 m. Average depth of floor, from 20 cm. above present ground surface to present ground surface.
>
> *Walls:* Similar to Room 1 in quality of construction, but blocks somewhat smaller and more uneven. Cross walls constructed of smaller sandstone blocks than exterior walls and consequently less shaping to individual pieces. Footed in places directly on bedrock. Maximum remaining height: 85 cm. Average width: 32 cm.
>
> *Entrance:* Probably through roof.
>
> *Floor:* Hard packed smooth red-brown sandy clay. Good condition. Slopes upward at southeast corner. Wall-floor juncture at right angles. No floor features. Fill placed in room to level of occupation surface.
>
> *Hearth:* None.
>
> *Roof:* Probably similar to Room 1.
>
> *Fill:* Similar to Room 1.
>
> *Material Culture:* One pebble pounder and two mano fragments in fill. Unmodified yellow pigment on floor.

[74]

FIGURE 39. *Ariz. D:11:2. Exterior wall of Room 1 abutting wall of Room 2. Note footing of wall on bedrock.*

Room 3 (Fig. 40)

Type of Structure: Rectangular surface mealing room.

Dimensions: East-West, 2.15 m.; North-South, 3.5 m. Average depth of floor, at present ground surface.

Walls: Similar to Rooms 1 and 2.

Entrance: Probably through roof.

Floor: Hard packed gray-brown clay with bedrock protruding in several areas. No preparation of floor. Several depressions in floor may have been for holding vessels or for storage. Eight partially slab-lined and partially clay-lined mealing bins cover most of the floor area. Two groups of three contiguous bins and a third group of two bins. No metates remaining in bins.

Hearth: None.

FIGURE 40. *Ariz. D:11:2. Room 3. Specialized mealing room with a total of eight mealing bins.*

Roof: Probably similar to Rooms 1 and 2.

Fill: Upper portion containing mainly sandstone blocks from fallen walls. Lower portion of hard packed red-brown, charcoal-flecked sand.

Material Culture: Ground concretion fragment, stone bead, worked stone disc, pecking stone, and two two-hand manos in fill. Twelve two-hand manos, a miniature dipper, piñon nuts (probably intrusive) in floor fill. A jar, fragments of ground stone, seven hammerstones, six waste flakes, two two-hand manos, one metate fragment, egg shell, and brown pigment on floor.

Architectural Summary

In spite of extensive testing, the only three structures at Ariz. D:11:2 are the three aforementioned continguous surface masonry rooms. The absence of a kiva or semi-subterranean mealing room is undoubtedly accounted for by the shallowness of the soil on the sandstone outcrop. It is only possible, in this immediate area, to build surface rooms unless underground structures were constructed by chipping through the sandstone.

The sequence of construction, observable by wall abutments and bonding, suggests Rooms 2 and 3 were built as a single unit with an abuting cross wall. Room 1 was apparently added on at some later date and abuts Room 2. There is a definite stylistic difference in masonry between Room 1 and the other structures, although all are of good quality block-type construction.

A wing wall abuts the southwest corner of Room 3 and extends 2 m. to the south. The function of this wing wall, which is similar to that of RBMV 551 (Beals *et al.* 1945), was probably to serve as protection against prevailing southwest winds. The area was most likely utilized as an outdoor work area.

The quality of masonry at Ariz. D:11:2 is far superior to that of any other excavated or surveyed site, which probably accounts for the unusual height of the remaining walls. Rather than the generally unshaped tabular sandstone pieces used in wall construction at other sites, the walls at Ariz. D:11:2 are primarily constructed of well-shaped sandstone blocks.

Other Excavations

Small test pits were dug in various places in an attempt to locate subsurface structures, such as mealing areas and a kiva, without success.

In addition, five test trenches were dug, mainly to the east downslope from the room blocks, in an attempt to determine the character and depth of the trash. The test trenches established that virtually all cultural material, that is, ceramic fragments and charcoal-stained soil, is entirely on the surface. The lack of ground cover and a resultant sheet erosion on the slopes suggests that at least some of the trash zone has eroded away.

Artifacts

Chipped Stone Artifacts

Chipped stone is even rarer at Ariz. D:11:2 than at other surveyed and excavated sites on Black Mesa as no artifacts of chipped stone were found. Six waste flakes, four of quartzite and two of chert, were found in various proveniences. One flake shows evidence of battering on the cortex suggesting that it might be a spall from a hammerstone.

Ground Stone Artifacts

Ground stone tools are plentiful especially those utilized for grinding corn. Almost all ground stone artifacts are well-worn or broken. All are made of the local Mesa Verde sandstone.

Of the twenty-two *manos* found at Ariz. D:11:2, nineteen are two-handed. The length of the two-hand manos range from 4.9 cm. to 22.61 cm. The width varies from 6 cm. to 12.8 cm. and the thickness ranges from 1.5 cm. to 6 cm. All the two-hand manos are sub-rectangular. Five manos have flat use surfaces and fourteen have convex use surfaces, eleven of which are faceted making two adjoining grinding surfaces. Six of the manos are unifacial and the remaining thirteen are bifacial. The manos range from fine to coarse grained sandstone. One mano has finger grips running the entire length of both leading and trailing edges. Three manos have red stain on the use surfaces indicating they were used for grinding pigment. One coarse grained mano fragment has three grinding surfaces, but it is too small to determine if it is a portion of a one- or two-hand mano. Of the two one-hand manos from the site, one, fashioned of fine-grain sandstone, is roughly rectangular in shape and measures 14.2 cm. in length, 7.8 cm. in width and 2.6 cm. in thickness. This bifacial mano is convex on one side with a diagonal transverse abrading groove across the entire width of the mano. The other side is slightly concave with a second longitudinal abrading groove situated only in the slightly concave center of the mano. The second one-hand mano of medium-grained sandstone is ovoid in shape and measures 10 cm. long, 9 cm. wide, and 5.7 cm. thick.

TABLE 8. *Mano types from Ariz. D:11:2.*

One-Hand Mano	2	Two-Hand Mano		20
Unifacial	0	Unifacial	6	
Bifacial	2	Bifacial	13	
Surface Convex	1	Multifacial	1	
Surface Flat	1	Faceted	11	
		Surface Convex	14	
		Surface Flat	5	
		Surfaces Convex and Flat	1	
		Total		22

A single *metate* fragment was found on the floor of Room 3. This medium-grained piece of sandstone is a section of a corner, indicating the metate was troughed and open at at least one end.

A ground sandstone *disc* was found in the fill of Room 3. The disc, which measures 2.8 cm. in diameter and 0.6 cm. in thickness, is unworked on the sides; the edges are ground smooth. The function of this artifact is unknown. One dark brown, fine-grained *stone bead*, with a diameter of 0.3 cm., was recovered. The bead is circular with a biconical hole drilled through the center. A crenoid stem was also found which has striations on one side suggesting its use as a bead. Two quartzite pecking stones, both measuring 6 cm. long and 4 cm. wide, were excavated. Both oval stones show evidence of pecking at both ends and along the edges. Seven hammerstones were situated on the floor of Room 3. They are all unmodified, fist-sized pieces of quartzite which show evidence of battering on many projecting edges. The length ranges from 5.2 cm. to 8.1 cm. and the width from 4.7 cm. to 6.7 cm. The shapes vary from irregular to ovoid. Their location on the floor of the mealing room suggests use as sharpening stones for manos and metates.

Ceramics

A little over one thousand sherds, as well as three whole or restorable vessels and three worked sherds, were found in all proveniences at Ariz. D:11:2.

The bulk of the pottery, over seven hundred sherds, consists of Tusayan Corrugated. The majority of the decorated pottery is Sosi and Dogoszhi Black-on-white with a relatively high incidence of Black Mesa Black-on-white. Of the three worked sherds, two are black-on-white, and the third is Tsegi Orange Ware. The two black-on-white worked sherds are slightly scooped. One is chipped to a circular shape 4.5 cm. in diameter; the other is ground to a sub-rectangular shape 2.5 cm. long and 1.9 cm. wide. The Tsegi Orange Ware sherd has been ground to a circular disc, measuring 3.5 cm. in diameter.

Of the three *whole* or *restorable vessels*, one is a miniature Tsegi Orange Ware dipper with a portion of the handle missing, found in Room 3. There is a black-on-red design on the interior with a red slip covering the exterior. A wide-mouthed Tusayan Gray Ware jar was found on the floor of Room 3. The finish is similar to Kiet Siel Gray, but the shape and handle is more reminiscent of Lino Gray, and may well fit into the Lino Tradition (Ambler *et al.* 1964:73). The finish is relatively rough with numerous coarse particles of temper visible but not dragged across the surface, as is typical with Lino Gray. The handle extends from the lip of the rim to the beginning of the maximum curvature of the vessel. This vessel was reconstructed from sherds. A whole, miniature Black Mesa Black-on-white pitcher was found on the surface of the slope where most of the surface sherds were recovered. Much of the design has faded from the body of the vessel. The bottom is indented.

Non-artifactual Material

Twenty-three piñon nuts were in the floor fill of Room 3 along the north wall. Since a living piñon tree had to be cut down near Room 3 during excavations, it is most likely that these nuts represent a rodent cache in recent times.

Two fragments of cream-white egg shell were also found in the floor fill of Room 3. Species identification has not been made.

Summary and Discussion

Ariz. D:11:2 is a three room surface masonry structure oriented northeast-southwest with a wing wall to the south. The masonry suggests two construction periods; nevertheless, the ceramic component indicates a short span of occupation dating in the A.D. 1050-1150 period and belonging to the late Pueblo II-early Pueblo III stage.

The function of this site is difficult to determine. Room 3, the unit with eight mealing bins and no hearth, was obviously a specialized food preparation area. The absence of hearths in Rooms 1 and 2 suggests their function was storage rather than habitation. If this is the case however, Ariz. D:11:2 has no habitable rooms. The absence of a kiva and a definite habitation unit produces the intrigu-

TABLE 9. *Provenience of pottery types from Ariz. D:11:2.*

Type	Surface	Strip Area 1	Test Trench 1	Test Trench 2	Test Trench 3	Test Trench 4
Tusayan White Ware	3	3	5	1	5	1
Black Mesa B/W	5			1	2	
Sosi B/W	19	3		1	4	1
Dogoszhi B/W	10	2			2	
Flagstaff B/W				1		
Unclassified B/W			1			
Shato Variety	1					
Tusayan Gray Ware	2	3			1	
Tusayan Corrugated	17	12	14	6	34	1
Moenkopi Corrugated	4					
Honani Tooled	1					
Tsegi Orange Ware	7	2		1		
Tusayan B/R	9		1		1	
Tusayan Polychrome		1				1
Total	77	26	21	11	49	4

ing possibility that the site was either only seasonally inhabited or functioned primarily as a storage and food preparation area. The numerous other sites in the immediate vicinity which ceramics indicate are roughly contemporaneous with Ariz. D:11:2 may well have served the religious and habitational functions for the people at this settlement. The contemporaneity of Ariz. D:11:2 with surrounding sites and possible inter-settlement relationships will only possibly be known upon excavation of a number of sites in the surrounding low valleys.

Ariz. D:11:11

Introduction

Ariz. D:11:11 is situated in a wide, sloping basin-like plain in which numerous other recorded and excavated sites (Ariz. D:11:12, Ariz. D:11:15) are located. This basin-like structure, which drains into the Moenkopi Wash, has probably the greatest concentration of sites of any comparable area yet recorded on northeastern Black Mesa. It is our hope that we can excavate as many sites as possible in this basin-like area in order to determine inter-settlement relationships. Most of the sites in the immediate vicinity belong to the late Pueblo II-early Pueblo III stage and the region appears ideal for study of possible economic and religious interaction between communities. The immediate environmental situation of Ariz.

[80]

TABLE 9. *Provenience of pottery types from Ariz. D:11:2.*

Test Trench 5	Exterior Walls	Room 1 Floor Fill	Room 1 Floor	Room 2 Fill	Room 2 Floor Fill	Room 2 Floor	Room 3 Fill	Room 3 Floor	Total
46	8	1	10	1	2	1	4	8	99
11	2		2	2			2	2	29
11	2	3	16			1	15	11	87
4	2	2	1				3	19	45
1							1	2	5
14	6			1			4	13	39
									1
20	1	1	2		1	1	4	10	46
116	29	70	113	5	136	118	38	28	737
5					3	1	2		15
									1
5							4	11	30
2			2				4	4	25
2		2	3			2	7		16
237	50	79	149	9	142	125	88	108	1,175

D:11:11 is on a gentle slope to the south approximately 150 m. east of the crest of a low hill, at an elevation of 6,500 feet. The main north-south Black Mesa road from Navajo National Monument to Piñon is approximately 200 m. northeast of this site. The settlement consists of two jacal structures: a subsurface mealing room, a kiva, and a small trash area, dating approximately in the A.D. 1050–1150 range (Fig. 41).

Geologically, Ariz. D:11:11 is on and in a thin layer of brown sand and clay alluvium overlying the Mesa Verde bedrock with numerous sandstone outcroppings at the crest of the hill to the north of the site. Arable land nearly surrounds the site, especially to the south where numerous depressions provide the soil and moisture for crops. The nearest source of permanent water is the main branch of the Upper Moenkopi Wash, which is approximately one-half mile to the south.

The environment of Ariz. D:11:11 is Upper Sonoran with the dominant plant cover chiefly various grasses and low bushes, such as sage brush, blue grama, sand dropseed, Indian rice grass, and cholla. Piñon and juniper trees are scattered on the upper slopes but none are presently growing near the site. The grasses only partially cover the sand and soil surfaces.

This settlement was excavated because of the immediate plans of Peabody Coal Company to place a large water storage structure over it.

Prior to excavation, the site appeared to consist of an L-shaped unit, with a kiva depression to the southeast. South and east of the kiva depression scatterings of sherds and masonry stone represented the trash deposits. A secondary bladed road, to the south and west of the kiva, probably removed a considerable portion of this trash area.

The low, L-shaped mound had numerous thin, partially shaped sandstone slabs scattered over the surface suggesting masonry rooms which had apparently been robbed for construction of a nearby settlement. Excavation soon indicated that these slabs were only on the surface and that the L-shaped mound was, in part, natural and, in part, back dirt from the excavation of the kiva. Excavation began by test trenching for the non-existing masonry rooms. Upon discovery of postholes, the test trenches were expanded into various strip areas. The kiva was located by the depression and excavated both by hand and with a backhoe. The mealing room was found by test trenching and excavated by hand. The refuse area was dissected by test trenches, which were later expanded into a strip area. No screening was done of any material.

Architecture

Structures 1 and 2 (Fig. 42)

Structures 1 and 2 are most likely jacal or ramada surface units. However, only portions of postholes and rotted posts were discovered so that only a sketchy description of the shape and dimensions can be made. It does appear that what has been called Structure 1 is circular and Structure 2 is rectangular. Several of the posts in both structures were charred near the old occupation surface, indicating they may have been destroyed by fire. Each structure contains a slab-lined hearth (Fig. 40). The hearth in Structure 1 is 95 cm. in diameter and 25 cm. deep. The bottom 10 cm. of fill contains light gray wood ash. The hearth in Structure 2 is 91 cm. in diameter and 25 cm. deep. The fill consists of light brown sand heavily charged with charcoal particles and ash. Two upright sandstone slabs northwest of this hearth may have served as a deflector. Because of the two slab-lined hearths it can be assumed that these structures, constructed of perishable materials, were domiciliary units.

There was no visible distinction between what is assumed to be the floor of Structures 1 and 2 and the old occupation surface surrounding the structure. The depth of overburden above the old occupation surface in Structures 1 and 2 varies from 10–28 cm. and the fill is loosely consolidated light brown sand with a small amount of charcoal sherds and pieces of sandstone. Fill is easily distinguishable from the old occupation surface, which is clayey and well-consolidated.

Mealing Room 1 (Fig. 44, 45)

Type of Structure: Semi-subsurface mealing room, irregularly ovoid in shape with a passage entry.

Dimensions: East-West, 3.35 m.; North-South, 2.05 m. Average depth of floor, 1 m. below present ground surface; 70 cm. from old occupation surface.

Walls: Formed by the native soil into which the structure was excavated. Upper portions of walls difficult to define because of erosion and slumpage after

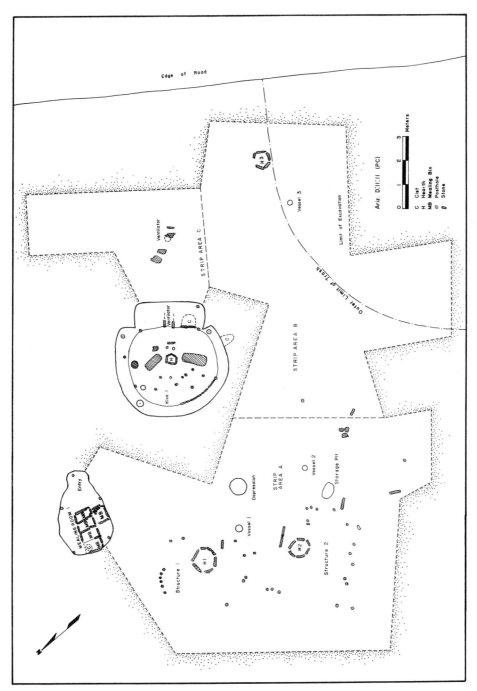

FIGURE 41. *Ariz. D:11:11. Plan view.*

[83]

FIGURE 42. *Ariz. D:11:11. Structures 1 and 2. Stakes represent postholes in ramada structures.*

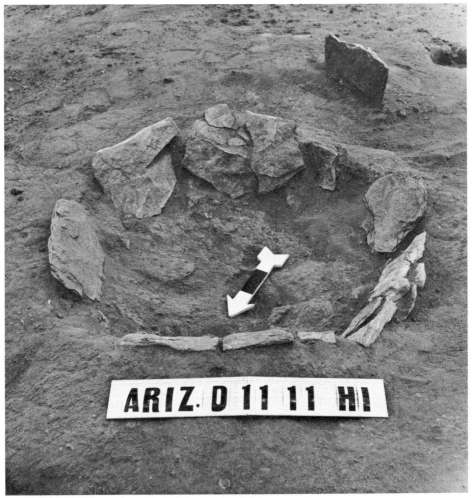

FIGURE 43. *Ariz. D:11:11. Hearth 1 inside of jacal structure.*

FIGURE 44. *Ariz. D:11:11. Mealing Room 1.*

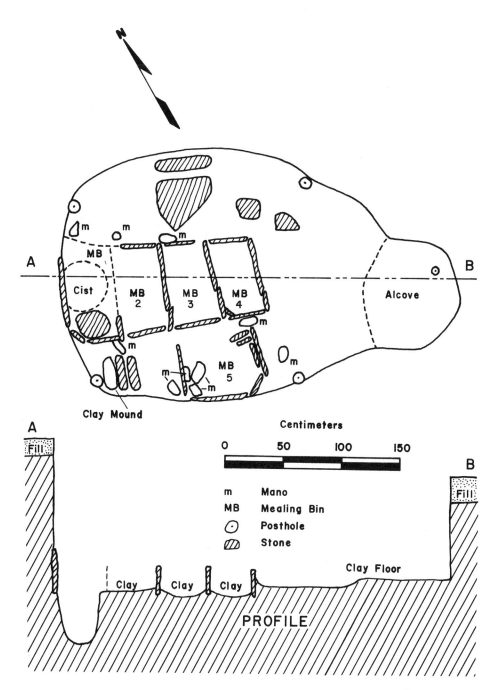

FIGURE 45. *Ariz. D:11:11. Mealing Room 1. Plan and profile.*

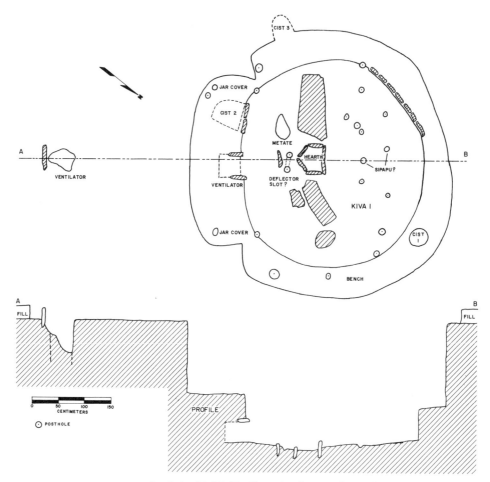

FIGURE 46. *Ariz. D:11:11. Kiva 1. Plan and profile.*

abandonment. No preparation of wall noted. Upper portions of wall probably of perishable material.

Entrance: Entry probably through the east-facing passage, which is raised 5–10 cm. above floor level. Length east-west, 90 cm.; width north-south, 68 cm. Entry passage may have served as ventilator shaft.

Floor: Unprepared, hard packed gray clay directly above bedrock. Uneven and curving up slightly to meet walls. Numerous unshaped sandstone slabs resting on floor, probably used in roof construction. Majority of floor occupied by mealing bins.

Postholes: Five holes, four with rotted remains of juniper, average 10 cm. in diameter and 12 cm. in depth. Four holes in structure proper, probably major roof support. Posts in a quadrilateral pattern against wall. One hole in floor of alcove.

[88]

FIGURE 47. *Ariz. D:11:11. Kiva 1. Hearth and ventilator shaft complex.*

All beams charred at floor level. Clay surrounds base of one post for support. Function of posthole in alcove unknown.

Hearth: None.

Mealing Bins: Five clay- and slab-lined bins average 40 cm. in width, 70 cm. in length, and 12 cm. below the clay floor. Four of the mealing bins are contiguous east to west. Grinding action to south. Fifth mealing bin against south wall, grinding action to east. No metates found in bins, but metate outlines visible in gray clay, which was used as mortar to hold metate in place.

Storage Pit: Slab-covered, unlined, under Mealing Bin 1. Diameter, 40 cm.; depth below floor, 50 cm.; fill, similar to mealing room fill. Pit probably covered and converted into mealing area.

Roof: Quadrilateral arrangement of roof supports suggests a rectangular plate on which horizontal timbers were placed. Sides probably formed by small poles presenting the appearance of a truncated pyramid. Burned beams and juniper bark from roof suggest no particular pattern.

Fill: Light brown sand flecked with charcoal to a depth of approximately 60 cm., 5–10 cm. above floor burned juniper bark and wood representing the burned roof. Floor fill not distinguishable from fill in color and texture. Along west wall, portions of native soil have slumped into fill.

Material Culture: Six pieces of red and two pieces of yellow pigment showing grinding on one or more surfaces; one quartzite polishing stone, one metate fragment, one waste flake, and three two-hand manos in fill. Seven manos and one metate fragment on floor. One sandstone abrading stone in storage pit.

Kiva 1 (Fig. 46, 47)

Type of Structure: Subterranean ceremonial room roughly circular with southern recess.

Dimensions: East-West, 4.85 m.; North-South, 5.25 m. Average depth of floor below present ground surface, 2.5 m., 2.2 m. below old occupation surface. Average depth of bench, 1.75 m. below present ground surface.

Walls: Vertical; dug into natural soil. One coat of dark brown clay plaster visible in patches; maximum height of plaster above floor, 57 cm. Portion of wall below west bench constructed of coursed masonry, which has slumped in parts. Masonry of thin, unshaped sandstone slabs with large amounts of mud mortar.

Bench: Constructed by leaving natural soil in place. Patches of plaster remaining similar to that on wall. Height varies from 60–75 cm. above floor; average width of bench, 20 cm.

Southern Recess: Unlined recess oriented to southeast. Length, 2.5 m.; width, 90 cm. Evidence of plaster similar to walls and bench.

Entrance: No evidence, probably opening in roof above hearth. No ladder sockets noted.

Floor: Poor condition; composed of native gray clay directly above bedrock. Two thin, brown plaster floors also observed in portion underlying a fourth gray clay floor in very poor condition. Often difficult to find various floor levels. Floor rounds up slightly to walls. Several large sandstone slabs, which may have rimmed room entry, directly on uppermost floor.

Postholes: Four postholes on bench, varying in diameter from 10–15 cm.; four secondary postholes against bench in a quadrilateral pattern, three with fragments of juniper in place. Ten small postholes in north section of kiva, some of which may be loom holes and two of which are candidates for the sipapu.

Hearth: Slab-lined, roughly rectangular, 60 cm. long and 50 cm. wide. Near center of structure. Light gray wood ash in bottom 15 cm. of fill.

Deflector: Two postholes 20 cm. south of hearth may have been the supports for a deflector constructed of perishable materials. Sandstone slab set in floor 10 cm. south of postholes projects 3 cm. above floor. There is no indication that this slab was broken off, suggesting it was not a deflector; its function is unknown.

Storage Cists: Cist 1 on north bench, diameter, 30 cm.; depth, 40 cm. Bell-shaped in profile. Cist 2 under southern recess, 40 cm. south of ventilator shaft opening. Opening to cist is slab-lined; opening, 50 cm. in diameter; depth, 54 cm. Cist 3 in south wall, 10 cm. above bench, 40 cm. deep. Rotting juniper poles suggest roof lining. No material culture, other than pot sherds, was found in fill of cists.

Roof: Numerous charred beams 5–20 cm. above floor in a pattern suggesting a cribbed-roof. No pilasters on bench. Cribbing may have begun at old occupation surface.

Fill: Varies from dark brown sand, with heavy charcoal flecking and large charcoal pieces, to orange-red eolian sand. Fill homogeneous throughout column. Numerous burned beams in fill indicate structure burned. No distinction between fill and floor fill except for a slight darkening in color near floor.

Ventilator: (Fig. 47) Square or rectangular opening 2 cm. above floor; width, 47 cm. Upper portions collapsed. Slab-lined on sides; slabs extend several centimeters into kiva. Ventilator opening at surface, 2.05 m. south of kiva. Ventilator shaft not completely excavated. Upright sandstone slab at south portion of ventilator opening on the surface probably served as wind deflector. Small, unshaped sandstone slab horizontal over ventilator openings served as lintel.

Material Culture: In fill, two manos, one hammerstone, two worked sherds and three bone awls; two stone jar covers and two worked sherds in floor fill; two pottery plates, a bone flesher, five waste flakes, a trough metate, and a Tusayan White Ware vessel on floor; two stone jar covers, an unfired clay pot, a core, and waste flake on bench.

Architectural Summary

The village pattern at Ariz. D:11:11 is similar in form to other early Pueblo III settlements on Black Mesa. The kiva is to the southeast of the two dwelling units and northeast of the dwellings, and north of the kiva is a semi-subterranean mealing room. The trash, much of which has been destroyed by a dirt road, is to the south and east of the habitation structures and kiva.

There is no indication of differing construction periods and all structures seem to have been abandoned when the inhabitants deserted the site. The number of large charcoal particles and charred beams, in both the mealing room and the kiva, indicate their destruction by fire.

The architectural surprise of the site is the lack of masonry habitation rooms and the low number (only two) of jacal or ramada structures. The question of the ratio of domiciliary units to kivas will be discussed later in this volume.

Refuse

Several test trenches were dug through the refuse area, which proved to be shallow, 10 cm. at its maximum depth, and relatively free of many sherds and organic staining. When the trenches proved relatively unrewarding, and manpower was available, the test trenches were expanded into a strip area. Because of the shallowness of the trash and the expansion of the sherd area to the south, I assume that the majority of the refuse was removed by the road cut to the south of the site. No stratigraphy was observed in any of the excavated portions of the refuse.

Other Excavations

For several reasons, trenches were expanded into strip areas. Strip A was excavated to the old occupation surface as soon as it was realized that we were dealing not with masonry structures but jacal units. The stripping technique was utilized in an attempt to isolate more posthole patterns. Strip B was utilized to excavate more of the refuse area and to increase our sherd count. Strip Area C was excavated to discover the ventilator shaft opening and to test for further structures to the northeast.

Stripping operations revealed several features. In Strip Area A, two restorable Tusayan Corrugated vessels were found in slight depressions unassociated with any structure. A large bowl-shaped depression of unknown function 70 cm. in diameter and 46 cm. deep was also found in Strip Area A. A third Tusayan Corrugated restorable vessel was found in a slight depression in Strip Area B as was Hearth 3. Hearth 3 is slab-lined, 68 cm. in diameter and 41 cm. deep. No ash was found in the fill.

Artifacts

Chipped Stone Artifacts

Typically, chipped stone artifacts and debitage are rare, forming only a very small percentage of the artifacts recovered.

Four stone jar covers were recovered from the kiva at Ariz. D:11:11. All are roughly circular pieces of thin sandstone which has been shaped by chipping along the edges. Upper and lower surfaces have not been worked. Diameters range from 13 cm. to 16.4 cm. and vary in thickness from 1 cm. to 1.5 cm. Two of the four covers were found in the floor fill of the kiva and the other two are on the surface of the southern recess, one in each southern corner. The location of these two artifacts near the corners, which are usually called jar covers, may indicate that these sandstone pieces were used as footings for roof support posts rather than as jar covers.

Two cores, both of quartzite, were found at the site. Both are approximately fist size, neither has any cortex remaining and there is no indication of a prepared striking platform. Three utilized flakes of quartzite were found, which have use scars along one edge; they range in size from 5.7 cm. to 3.2 cm. in length, and 5.3 cm. to 2 cm. in width. Seven waste flakes of chalcedony, chert, and quartzite were found scattered throughout the site. These flakes show no evidence of usage.

Ground Stone Artifacts

Of the forty-two *manos* found at Ariz. D:11:11, only four are whole and these are extremely worn. The maximum length of the complete manos is 25 cm. and the minimum is 10.9 cm. The maximum width is 12.9 cm. and the minimum is 6.5 cm. All the manos are sub-rectangular in shape and range from fine- to coarse-grained sandstone. Three of the manos are of the one-hand variety, ranging in length from 7.5–9.2 cm. and in width from 6.4–7.8 cm. Two of the manos are rectangular and the third is ovoid. All three are bifacial and fashioned of fine-grained sandstone. Details on the manos are found in Table 10.

TABLE 10. *Mano types from Ariz. D:11:11.*

One-Hand Mano		3	Two-Hand Mano		39
Unifacial			Unifacial	21	
Bifacial	3		Bifacial	18	
Surface Convex	3		Faceted	24	
Surface Flat			Surface Convex	35	
			Surface Flat	4	
			Total	42	

In contrast to the large number of manos, only four metate fragments were found at Ariz. D:11:11. Three of the fragments are of the trough variety, opened at least on one end, and the remaining metate is of the flat variety. Two of the trough metates and the flat metate were fashioned of fine-grained white sandstone, while the third trough metate was of a coarse-grained ground sandstone.

Eight *miscellaneous* pieces of *ground sandstone* were found in various proveniences. They are of such fragmentary nature that their function cannot be determined, although some of them are probably fragments of manos and metates. Two small pieces show evidence of the grinding of red pigment. A piece of ground calcite, roughly ovoid 3.1 cm. in diameter with several ground facets, was also found but its function is unknown.

An ovoid, partially finished pendant of pink siltstone measuring 4.9 cm. in length, 3.9 cm. in width, and .03 cm. in thickness was found. The edges were chipped to shape and then partially ground. Striations from grinding appear on one face. Near one edge is a conical hole which only partially penetrates the width of the disc.

Miscellaneous Stone Artifacts

Eight *hammerstones* were recovered from Ariz. D:11:11, three of which are petrified wood, four are quartzite and the eighth of an unidentified material. In shape, the hammerstones range from ovoid to roughly rectangular and are unshaped. They exhibit battering on one or more surfaces. Three of the hammerstones have numerous large chips and flakes removed as a result of hammering. Length range from 6 cm. to 11.5 cm., and widths from 5 cm. to 9.2 cm.

Six quartzite pebbles were found in various proveniences and are the type of unmodified stones which appear highly smoothed and polished and are often called *polishing stones*. Although these pebbles have a high luster on at least one surface, there is no indication that these stones were actually used as polishing instruments. They vary in length from 3.9 cm. to 6.4 cm., and in width from 2.9 cm. to 5.1 cm.

[93]

TABLE 11. *Provenience of pottery types from Ariz. D:11:11.*

Types	Surface	Strip Area 1	Strip Area 2	Hearth 1	Hearth 2	Storage Pit
Tusayan White Ware	15	306	343	3	2	10
Black Mesa B/W	1	62	54		3	3
Sosi B/W	20	403	300		1	15
Dogoszhi	7	163	209		2	4
Flagstaff B/W	1	45	51			
Unclassified B/W	8	344	459			13
Shato Variety		38	33			
Tusayan Gray Ware	1	146	160			
Honani Tooled		3	3			
Tusayan Corrugated	52	1886	2105	11	6	22
Moenkopi Corrugated	7	214	256	5		
O'Leary Tooled		6	10			
Tsegi Orange Ware	1	86	77			1
Medicine B/R		6	2			
Tusayan Polychrome		4				1
Tusayan B/R		60	48			2
Total	113	3734	4077	19	14	71

Nine small articles of *pigment* were recorded at Ariz. D:11:11. Five are yellow ocher from the fill of Strip Area 1, and the remainder, from various proveniences, are red pigment. Only three pieces show grinding facets. All are irregular in shape and none exceed 1.2 cm. in length.

Ceramics

The total number of pottery fragments from Ariz. D:11:11 total 9,772, which is relatively high considering the small number of habitation units and the thinness of the trash zone.

Tusayan Gray Ware predominates with a total of almost 6,000 sherds; and of these, almost 5,000 are Tusayan Corrugated. Sosi and Dogoszhi Black-on-white are the predominant decorated pieces, with Black Mesa and Flagstaff Black-on-white showing up in a much smaller quantity.

Four whole or partially restored vessels were recovered from the site. One is a Tusayan Corrugated jar, partially restored, that was found on the floor of the ramada area. The rim and upper portion of the vessel are missing; the height, as restored, is 19.3 cm. and the diameter is 24.5 cm. An almost whole Tusayan White

TABLE 11. *Provenience of pottery types from Ariz. D:11:11.*

Mealing Room 1 Fill	Mealing Room 1 Floor Fill	Mealing Room 1 Floor	Mealing Room 1 Sub-floor	Mealing Room 1 Meal'g Bin	Kiva 1 Fill	Kiva 1 Floor Fill	Kiva 1 Floor	Kiva 1 Recess	Total
76	23			3	14	4	1	1	801
14	1	1	1	2		2			144
71	24	2		4	17	4		1	862
63	23	3		7	7	7			495
10	5				3	2		1	118
118	28	1		8	21	16	7	2	1025
9	1				3	2		1	87
66	13			3	7	6		1	403
									6
531	155	8	2	24	40	66	24	4	4936
51	25	1		11	9		5	1	585
	1								17
26	11	2	1	1	8	1	8		223
	1				1				10
1	1				1				8
16	2	2		1	2	4	2		138
1043	313	20	4	64	130	112	47	11	9772

Ware bowl was discovered on the floor of Kiva 1. There is no design present on the vessel; however, there are both interior and exterior fire clouds. The bowl is not slipped. The maximum diameter of the bowl is 21 cm., the height is 16.5 cm. Two fragmentary Tusayan Gray Ware plates were found on the floor of Kiva 1. Both are saucer-shaped, with flattened bottoms. One has a Tusayan Corrugated exterior, and is 10.3 cm. in diameter, although a portion of the rim is missing. The other plate is a plain gray ware, with a scraped and pitted exterior measuring 10.1 cm. in diameter. The plates are of the type A. J. Lindsay (personal communication) is calling Tsegi Corrugated.

Only thirteen of the pottery fragments were classified as *worked sherds*. Four of the worked sherds are fragmentary and their original form is uncertain. The remaining worked sherds are ground into roughly oblong form, varying in length from 10.5 cm. to 2.8 cm. They are all scoop shaped with edges ground smooth to varying degrees. Some of these worked sherds may have been used to scrape the inside of vessels during manufacture, since the widest end of the worked sherd is usually the most worn portion. Other larger worked sherds may have served as plates or scoops. One of the sherds is an undecorated Tusayan White Ware, seven are Dogoszhi Black-on-white, two Black Mesa Black-on-white, one Flagstaff Black-on-white, one Sosi Black-on-white, and one unclassified Tusayan Black-on-white ware.

Data for whole and restorable vessels at Ariz. D:11:11 is given in Table 12.

TABLE 12. *Whole and restorable vessels from Ariz. D:11:11.*

Type	Form	Maximum Diameter	Rim Diameter	Volume	Height	Provenience	Figure
Gray Ware	Plate	15.1 cm.	15.1 cm.		3.0 cm.	Kiva 1, floor	9, A
Gray Ware	Plate	13.3 cm.	13.3 cm.	132 ml.	2.8 cm.	Kiva 1, floor	9, B
Tusayan White Ware	Bowl	22.4 cm.	22.3 cm.		11.5 cm.	Kiva 1, floor	
Gray Ware	Miniature Jar	2.9 cm.	2.8 cm.	2 ml.	0.9 cm.	Strip 1	

Bone

Three splinter bone *awls* were recovered from the fill of the mealing room. All are badly weathered bone fragments with no articular surfaces remaining. Though badly weathered, all appear to have been ground to a sharp point. One awl is 11.6 cm. in length, the second is 7.4 cm., and the third is 8.3 cm. in length.

One bone *flesher* was found at Ariz. D:11:11. The short flesher is a split long bone 6.7 cm. long and 2.6 cm. wide. The proximal end is broken and partially ground smooth. The distal, or working, end is rounded and ground to a rounded edge. The interior edge of the split bone is ground flat. There are numerous transverse striations and two shallow transverse grooves on the exterior surface near the proximal edge of the flesher. These grooves and striations may be the result of the hafting of the short flesher to a wood handle.

Shell

A fragmentary glycymeris shell *bracelet* was in the fill of Strip Area A. The fragment is 3 cm. long and 0.6 cm. wide. It appears to represent about one-sixth of the original bracelet. All of the surfaces of the bracelet are ground smooth and highly polished. One edge appears to have been partially burned.

Summary and Discussion

In spite of initial impressions prior to excavations, Ariz. D:11:11 consists architecturally of only two ramada or jacal structures, a subsurface mealing room, a kiva, and a trash area. The small number of domiciliary units suggests that the site was occupied by no more than an extended family or two, even if the kiva was also used, in part, as a habitation structure. No burials were found at the site but they may have been removed by road construction to the south of the site.

Ceramics indicate the settlement was occupied by Kayenta Anasazi in the A.D. 1050–1150 range.

The small amount of animal bones and the large numbers of mano fragments, along with the mealing rooms, suggest a dependence by the inhabitants of Ariz. D:11:11 primarily on plant foods, both wild or domesticated. The nearby water supply of Upper Moenkopi Wash and the many alluvial filled flats and basins in the immediate vicinity, as well as a Navajo squash field 200 m. from the site, suggest that the immediate environment was ideal for agriculture. Certainly hunting must have played a secondary role.

The thinness of the undisturbed trash and the absence of burials, as well as the small size of the settlement, suggest a relatively short occupation of perhaps no more than five or ten years. The worn and fragmentary condition of the manos and the absence of metates in the mealing bins suggest an orderly abandonment of the site, in spite of the fact that both the mealing room and the kiva were burned.

The relationship of Ariz. D:11:11 to other surrounding and presumably contemporaneous communities will have to await excavation of these sites. At present no economic, religious, or social ties between these sites can be distinguished.

Ariz. D:11:8

Introduction

Ariz. D:11:8 (Fig. 48), situated on the crest of a low knoll in the basin-like area near the Peabody Coal Company preparation plant, was first observed from the air during the initial survey. It is within this alluvial-filled basin-like structure, which drains south to Moenkopi Wash, that other sites were excavated, such as Ariz. D:11:11, Ariz. D:11:12, and Ariz. D:11:15. Ariz. D:11:11 lies approximately 1600 feet to the west of Ariz. D:11:8. Two large unexcavated sites, Ariz. D:11:13 and Ariz. D:11:29, which were not observed during the helicopter survey, lie within 15 m. to the north and 15 m. to the south of Ariz. D:11:8. Cultural affiliation is with the Kayenta Anasazi and the site is classified as late Pueblo II-early Pueblo III, i.e., similar to surrounding sites.

The immediate environmental and geological setting is similar to the other sites described in preceding sections of this report, especially Ariz. D:11:11. Backhoe trenches, as deep as twelve feet at this site, revealed loosely consolidated light-brown sand. Bedrock was not reached.

This site, which consists of a single masonry room, appeared prior to excavation to consist of one masonry surface room and a few scattered sherds; no depression was noted. I had assumed that the room might be a storage area for people dwelling in jacal structures or in associated pithouses. Backhoe trenching, in all directions from the masonry room, revealed no additional features. It seems, consequently, that the room is associated with another nearby site.

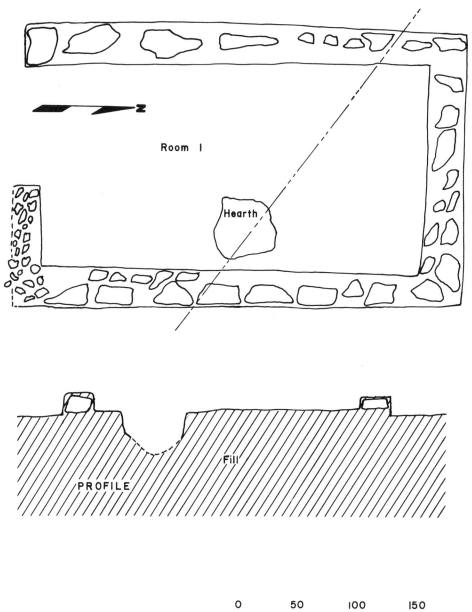

Room 1

Hearth

Fill

PROFILE

FIGURE 48. *Ariz. D:11:8. Plan and profile.*

[98]

FIGURE 49. *Ariz. D:11:8. Room 1.*

Architecture

Room 1 (Fig. 49)

Type of Structure: Rectangular surface dwelling.

Dimensions: East-West, 2.21 m.; North-South, 3.75 m.

Walls: Two courses of minimally-shaped sandstone slabs, one or two slabs in width, at northeast corner; east and west walls, a single course of sandstone slabs; only small, scattered pieces of sandstone remaining at southeast corner. Southwest portion of wall missing. Walls may have been robbed of well-shaped pieces to construct rooms at other nearby sites.

Entrance: None noted; possibly at southwest corner or through roof.

Floor: Hard packed reddish-brown native sand and clay. Surface uneven, much rodent and root activity. Unprepared and difficult to determine because disturbed soil continues in places below floor.

Hearth: Unlined, irregularly shaped pit; near midpoint of room 15 cm. from east wall. Fire-reddened on east and west sides. East-West, 52 cm.; North-South, 47 cm. No ash in fill.

Roof: Probably beams laid horizontally across upper courses of wall.

Fill: Red-brown sand charged with small charcoal particles. Disturbed soil

[99]

continues below floor to depth of approximately 60 cm. near the north and west sides. Floor fill indistinguishable from fill.

Material Culture: A single one-hand mano in fill.

Other Excavations

A backhoe was used unsuccessfully to test for subsurface structures and a trash deposit. Nearly all cultural material is on the surface and no specific refuse deposit area could be determined.

An area south and west of Room 1 (Strip A) was excavated to the old occupation surface in an unsuccessful attempt to discover jacal structures.

Artifacts

Lithic Artifacts

A single one-hand mano fashioned of medium-grained sandstone was found in the fill of Ariz. D:11:8. It is ovoid with two convex use surfaces. The mano is 9.3 cm. long and 8.4 cm. wide. A medium-grained sandstone metate fragment was found in Strip Area A. The fragments suggest the metate was of the trough variety, open on at least one end. Three miscellaneous pieces of sandstone, which evidence grinding, may be portions of broken manos or metates.

One cylindrical, petrified wood hammerstone was found in the Strip Area. Pounding scars are visible on both ends. Three chert waste flakes were also found in the Strip Area.

Ceramics

A surprisingly large number of sherds were found at Ariz. D:11:8, considering the smallness of the excavated area and the scarceness of artifacts. The ceramic complex, which is dominated by Tusayan White and Gray Ware, has the typical late Pueblo II-early Pueblo III Kayenta Anasazi make-up. The decorated black-on-whites are dominated by Sosi Black-on-white followed by Dogoszhi and Black Mesa Black-on-white. No intrusive sherds or whole vessels were found.

Summary and Discussion

Ariz. D:11:8 held few surprises, consisting solely of a one room masonry structure, which was apparently robbed for its building materials. The site, which dates in the A.D. 1050–1150 range, was initially assumed to be a discrete settlement or probably more accurately, a habitation room, may well instead be related to either Ariz. D:11:13 to the north or Ariz. D:11:29 to the south. Both of these neighboring sites are much larger and ceramically, at least, suggest contemporaneity with Ariz. D:11:8. Since no jacal structures were found nor an associated kiva, the best explanation of the function of Room 1 is that it is an outlying room to one of the larger nearby sites. It is worth noting here that both of these larger sites have tremendous trash deposits but no masonry is visible, suggesting extensive jacal structures.

TABLE 13. *Provenience of pottery types from Ariz. D:11:8.*

Type	Surface	Strip A	Test Trench	Room Fill	Floor	Sub-Floor	Hearth	Total
Tusayan White Ware	12	19	18	2		1	2	54
Kana-a B/W	3							3
Black Mesa B/W	25	7	3			2	1	38
Sosi B/W	6	27	8	2	4	1		48
Dogoszhi B/W	7	8	6		2		2	25
Flagstaff B/W		1						1
Unclassified B/W	1	15	9	5	1			31
Tusayan Gray Ware	5	14	5	1	3	1		29
Honani Tooled		4			1			5
Tusayan Corrugated	2	158	31	6	16	5		218
Moenkopi Corrugated	11	41	10	21	3	3	2	91
Coconino Gray	3							3
Kana-a Gray	9							9
Tsegi Orange Ware		8	5	4	1		3	21
Tusayan B/R	7	10	1		1	1		20
Unclassified		1						1
Tusayan Polychrome							2	2
Total	91	313	96	41	32	14	12	599

Ariz. D:11:15

Introduction

Ariz. D:11:15 is a late Pueblo II Kayenta Anasazi site with several habitation rooms, a kiva, and a small refuse area (Fig. 50).

This small site was not excavated during the summer field school nor was the excavation sponsored by Peabody Coal Company, as were the other excavations. The monies for excavation were provided by the Black Mesa Pipeline Co., Inc. Ariz. D:11:15 is in the area of the coal crushing plant and pumping station, which the latter company is constructing.

The site was first recorded by Euler and Gumerman in March, 1968, and revisited on November 13, 1968, in order to prepare a cost estimate for Black Mesa Pipeline. Excavations were begun on November 15 and concluded on November 20. Six Navajos and five students were employed as laborers.

Before excavation, the site was indicated by a low mound of sandstone rubble suggesting several masonry rooms, a kiva depression to the southeast, and a small trash area partially cut by a dirt road to the southeast of the kiva depression.

The settlement is situated on a slight knoll in the same basin-like structure that Ariz. D:11:11, Ariz. D:11:8, and Ariz. D:11:12, other excavated sites, are located. A small, north-south trenching arroyo debouching into Moenkopi Wash

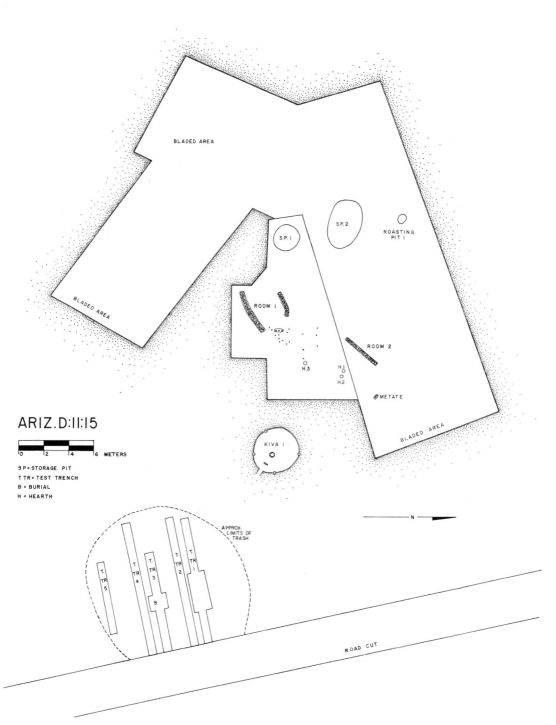

FIGURE 50. *Ariz. D:11:15. Plan view.*

[102]

FIGURE 51. *Ariz. D:11:15. Preparations for excavation in November.*

is heardward cutting approximately 20 m. to the east of the settlement. The low area, through which the arroyo is presently cutting, is an alluvial-filled depression and may have been utilized as an agricultural area. The Moenkopi Wash, less than one-half mile to the southeast, is the nearest source of water.

The immediate environmental situation is similar to that described for Ariz. D:11:11. The knoll, within the basin where the site is located, is a loosely consolidated tan-brown sand, presumably overlying Mesa Verde sandstone, although bedrock was never reached during the excavations. The sand is held in place by a relatively dense stand of sagebrush, Indian rice grass, grama grass, and Opuntia. No piñon or juniper trees are situated in the immediate vicinity, although they are visible on surrounding low hills.

Excavation was accomplished by hand and with the use of a road grader. The road grader was used to blade areas after all stripping was accomplished by hand, and it was assumed that there was little chance of revealing additional features. That this assumption was wrong is demonstrated by the discovery of Room 2 which was uncovered by the road grader. Because of the presumed masonry rooms, excavation was started by test trenching toward the rubble. When it became obvious that the rooms were robbed and only the footing of the walls remained, the test trenches were expanded into three strip areas designated A through C. A test trench was placed through the kiva depression to delineate the walls. The fill was then removed by hand. Excavation was hampered the first few days by a several inch deep snow cover and temperatures which were below freezing (Fig. 51).

Architecture

Room 1 (Fig. 52)

Type of Structure: Rectangular masonry surface dwelling or storage room.

Dimensions: Approximate East-West, 3.7 m.; North-South, 2.7 m. Floor on old occupation surface.

Walls: North and south walls of thin, unshaped pieces of tabular masonry. North wall maximum of five courses. South wall maximum of six courses and tumbled outward. Maximum remaining height of walls, 27 cm. No mortar or plaster noted. Few masonry slabs, with exception of wall stones *in situ*, suggesting robbing by later occupants of the area. No footing noted. Slabs placed directly on old occupation surface. Curvature of masonry walls probably due to collapse of walls and disturbance after abandonment. East wall probably jacal. Four postholes at right angles to masonry walls. Three of four postholes in trench, indicating jacal rather than ramada type wall. No evidence of any wall on west side.

Entrance: None noted. Possibly on west side or through roof.

Floor: Native soil. No preparation noted. No difference noted between old occupation surface within the structure or outside of it. Old occupation surface uneven and difficult to delineate.

Hearth: None.

Roof: Probably beams laid in a north-south direction across uppermost course of masonry.

Fill: Aeolian sand stained dark gray from humic material. Fill consistent throughout column. No differentiation noted between fill and floor fill. Few sandstone slabs from wall fall.

Material Culture: Sandstone abrader, two worked sherds, and two two-hand manos in fill.

Room 2 (Fig. 53)

Type of Structure: Surface masonry dwelling or storage room. Shape indeterminate because only footing for one wall remains.

Dimensions: Maximum length of wall footing, 2.87 m. Dimensions of room not determinable.

Walls: All walls apparently robbed of sandstone for construction of structure elsewhere. Only footing for one wall remains. Footing of small fitted sandstone

[104]

FIGURE 52. *Ariz. D:11:15. Room 1.*

chunks set directly on old occupation surface. Maximum height, 10 cm.; average width, 28 cm. Room constructed on slight slope indicating use of footing to level one wall prior to setting of coursed masonry.

Entrance: Indeterminate.

Floor: Indistinguishable from old occupation surface so that it is not possible to tell on which side of the wall footing the floor is located. Since the slope is to the south, and the wall footing is to compensate for the slope, the floor is probably to the north of the footing.

Hearth: None.

Fill: Portion of fill to top of wall footing removed by road grader. Remainder of fill light brown charcoal stained sand indistinguishable from other fill at site above occupation surface. No floor fill distinguishable.

Material Culture: No artifacts, other than sherds, in fill or on old occupation surface to the north and south of wall footing.

[105]

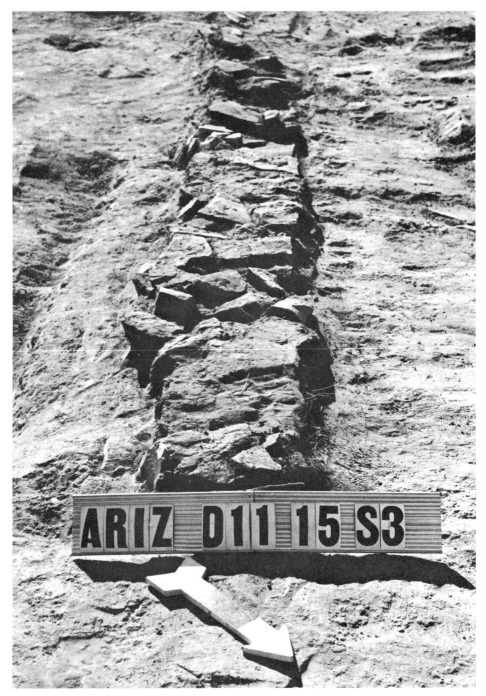

FIGURE 53. *Ariz. D:11:15. Footing for wall of Room 2.*

FIGURE 54. *Ariz. D:11:15. Hearth and ventilator shaft complex.*

Kiva 1 (Fig. 54, 55, 56)

Type of Structure: Oval subsurface ceremonial room.

Dimensions: East-West, 2.98 m.; North-South, 3.1 m. Average depth of floor, 2.67 m. below present ground surface; about 2 m. below old occupation surface.

Walls: Sandstone masonry to a maximum height of 1.15 m. Two distinct styles of masonry. Majority of masonry composed of long, thin tabular pieces of sandstone with great variation in size, including some blocky pieces of sandstone. Individual pieces vary from 10 cm. to 65 cm. thick. Considerable use of brown clay mortar. A 2 m. section of west wall between two roof support posts is composed of very small (often less than 0.5 cm. thick) sandstone chunks; even smaller pieces sometimes used as chinking. Less brown clay mortar than major section of wall. Gaps in masonry at four places for roof support posts, which are partially set behind walls. One thick coat, up to 1 cm., of brown clay plaster on walls

FIGURE 55. *Ariz. D:11:15. Kiva 1. Wall detail demonstrating differences in masonry on either side of posthole.*

remaining in patches. Exterior surface of plaster slightly smoke blackened. No
bench encircling kiva walls. Wall in north section has tilted in considerably since
abandonment.

    Entrance: Probably through roof above hearth. No ladder holes in floor.

    Floor: Brown clay plaster mixed with small particles of charcoal. Plaster 1
cm. thick in places and very thin in other areas. Totally eroded in places. Cross
section of floor slightly dish shaped. Floor rounds up slightly to meet walls. Inverted neck of jar plastered into floor 1.34 m. north of hearth, apparently used for
storage. Broken neck of jar beveled smooth at floor level. Bottom of this unusual
storage area unlined. No sipapu found, but northwest section of floor eroded.

    Postholes: Four major roof support posts in a quadrilateral pattern set par-

FIGURE 56. *Ariz. D:11:15. Kiva 1. Neck of jar plastered into floor and used as a storage area.*

tially in back of masonry walls. Fragments of juniper posts remain. Average diameter, 12 cm.; average depth of postholes below floor, 18 cm.

Hearth: Circular, 50 cm. in diameter; 12 cm. deep. Basin-shaped in cross section. Lined with plaster-like floor, but baked hard. Bottom 2 cm. of fill light gray wood ash. Clean blow sand, 3 cm. deep, above wood ash suggesting a period of abandonment before collapse of roof.

Deflector: Sandstone slab deflector 80 cm. from ventilation opening. Broken off at top; remaining height, 30 cm.; width, 33 cm.; and thickness, 1 cm.

Ventilator: Opening square; 30 cm. on a side in southeast wall. Opening 23 cm. from floor and faced with sandstone slab. Roof and side of shaft slab lined. Floor of native soil. Entire ventilation shaft not excavated and opening at old occupation surface not found.

Roof: Quadrilateral position of roof support posts suggests a rectangular plate on which beams are laid vertically. Side poles probably leaned against rectangular plate forming a truncated pyramid.

Fill: Deposited by wind and water action. Majority of fill well-consolidated sandy clay. Some calcium deposition forming. Numerous pockets of clean blow sand becoming more prevalent towards floor. Near wall at floor juncture blow sand up to 15 cm. deep, suggesting sand blew in before roof collapsed. Large number of sandstone slabs from upper courses of wall in fill. Very few sherds and charcoal flecking in fill. No distinction between fill and floor fill.

Material Culture: A maul, two worked sherds, and seven manos in fill; metate fragment used as arrow shaft straightener and six worked sherds in floor fill; an arrow shaft straightener, worked sherd, and mano on floor.

Storage Pit 1

Located 3.85 m. northeast of Room 1. Dimensions East-West, 2 m.; North-South, 2.26 m. Depth from present ground surface, 83 cm.; from old occupation surface, 62 cm. Fill of brown-red sand heavily charged with small charcoal flecks. Fill consistent throughout column. Pit basin-shaped in cross section. Walls and floor unprepared and very uneven.

Storage Pit 2

Located 2 m. north of Storage Pit 1. Dimensions East-West, 3.5 m.; North-South, 3 m. Depth from present ground surface, 40 to 54 cm.; from old occupation surface, 30 to 44 cm. Walls and floor uneven and unprepared. Slightly basin-shaped in cross section. Fill of well-consolidated, brown-red sand with small amounts of charcoal. Difficult to tell fill from culturally sterile soil.

Roasting Pit 1

Located 2.75 m. south of Storage Pit 2. Dimensions East-West, 92 cm.; North-South, 85 cm.; 45 cm. deep. Oval in shape. Walls slope slightly outward; bottom flat. Walls and floor unprepared but burned hard. Fill of red-brown sand with large amounts of charcoal. Bottom 4 cm. of fill mainly large pieces of charcoal and ash.

Hearths

Three hearths were located between Rooms 1 and 2 and the kiva. All three hearths are roughly circular with diameters of 43 cm., 50 cm., and 54 cm. All are basin-shaped in cross section and unlined. The respective depths are 38 cm., 40 cm., and 53 cm. No ash or large pieces of charcoal were found in the fill of the hearths.

Architectural Summary

Details of domestic architecture are difficult to distinguish because of the robbed masonry. Remains of two masonry rooms were found, one of which has at least one jacal wall. Neither of these rooms has a hearth and no determination can be made if they are domestic or storage rooms. The two oval storage pits at Ariz. D:11:15 suggest the rooms may have been domestic structures.

A series of postholes north of Room 1 probably indicates a jacal or ramada structure, but no definite pattern to the postholes could be distinguished. The search for a subsurface mealing room, in the usual position northeast of the kiva, was unsuccessful.

The oval kiva has few distinctive features except for the relatively high quality of masonry, the recessed roof supports, and the fact that the kiva was not burned. This is the only unburned kiva excavated during the 1968 season.

Refuse

The relatively small refuse midden to the southeast of the architectural units was dissected by five 50 cm. wide test trenches in an effort to increase artifact recovery, discover burials, and obtain an indication of the depth and composition of the trash. In two instances, the test trenches were expanded to explore the possibilities of a burial; in one case, successfully.

The trash, now represented by humic stained soil, sherds, and pieces of worked and unworked stone, has a maximum depth of 55 cm. near the center and gradually thins out near the edges. The eastern extremity of the midden has been destroyed by a dirt road. It appears that only a small part of the total trash was destroyed by the road construction.

Artifacts

Chipped Stone Artifacts

Except for one fragmentary, dark gray chert *projectile point,* no chipped stone artifacts were excavated from the site. The projectile point was located in the fill of Strip B. The tip end and one spur of the point are missing. The edges are parallel and bifacially flaked. The base is slightly concave. The length of the point is 2.2 cm. and the width, 1.4 cm.

Ground Stone Artifacts

Nineteen two-hand *manos* and two one-hand manos were excavated at the site; rather a low number compared to other excavated sites on Black Mesa. Seven of the two-hand manos were located in the fill of Kiva 1, the remainder came from the trash mound test trenches and Strip Areas A and B.

The two-hand manos are mainly fine-grain white-to-gray sandstone, with two constructed from coarse grain sandstone. The fragmentary manos range in length from 5.6 cm. to 13.5 cm., and in width from 4.2 cm. to 11 cm.; four manos are whole and range in length from 18.9 to 23.7 cm., and in width from 8.9 cm. to 12.8 cm. Ten of the manos have one use surface, and eight are non-faceted. The remaining nine manos exhibit two use surfaces and all but three are non-faceted. The three faceted manos show facets on only one side. Edges of all the manos are chipped and then ground to shape.

The two one-hand manos are fine and medium grained sandstone. They are 11.4 cm. and 11.5 cm. in length, and both are 7.1 cm. in width. The shapes are ovoid and rectangular. Both are non-faceted, with two use surfaces. The secondary grinding surface, in both cases, shows evidence of only slight usage.

One whole *metate,* found on the surface, and one fragmentary metate, excavated from the fill of Test Trench 3, were recovered. Both are fine grain, tan-white sandstone. The whole metate is of the open end trough variety. It is 43.6 cm. in length and 34.2 cm. in width and is sub-rectangular in shape. The grinding surface is slightly concave, and a small portion is exfoliated at one end. Edges are chipped and ground to shape. The dorsal surface is flat, but unworked. The metate fragment is rectangular and was found in two pieces with both ends missing. The length is 8.9 cm. and width is 7.8 cm. One side is ground and sloping; the ground surface is concave. The metate was of a trough variety, but neither end is present.

Double utilization of a sandstone artifact as a metate and *arrow shaft straightener* was discovered in the floor fill of Kiva 1. The fragment is trapezoid in shape, 12.3 cm. in length and 5.6 cm. in width. One surface is ground flat and is apparently a part of a metate. The opposing surface is unworked except for a transverse groove; all edges are fragmented. The tool was first used as a metate, and after fracturing, was made into an arrow shaft straightener. Another fine grain sandstone arrow shaft straightener was found on the floor of Kiva 1. The sandstone is irregular in form, although it is partially shaped; it is 14.1 cm. long and 13.1 cm. wide. It is smoothed on one side, with two deep parallel grooves running the length of the side. The artifact is partially smoke blackened.

A fine-grain red sandstone *abrader* was excavated from the Strip A fill. It is roughly rectangular in shape; 28.4 cm. in length and 10 cm. wide. The use surface is ground smooth and is slightly convex. The opposing surface is flat and unworked.

One *maul,* fashioned from fine-grain gray sandstone, was found in the fill of Kiva 1. It is 12.9 cm. long and 8.6 cm. wide. The bit and poll ends are both ground and rounded. The bit end, however, is indented from use. The maul is full-grooved. One side is ground extremely smooth, with a slight lip on one edge suggesting that it was fashioned from a metate fragment.

Miscellaneous Ground Stone

Three *hammerstones* were excavated from various proveniences. They range in length from 5.8 cm. to 6.8 cm. and in width from 4.3 cm. to 5.7 cm.; all are whole. Two are quartzite, and one is a hard metamorphic rock. All are roughly oval and unworked except for pounding scars. Heavy usage is indicated on each, with primary flakes removed from one due to pounding.

An oval, fine-grain reddish sandstone *pendant,* 2.8 cm. long and 2.2 cm. wide, was discovered in the fill of Test Trench 4. One surface is almost entirely exfoliated. A conical hole is located near the edge. All edges are beveled flat. One piece of worked red siltstone was found in Strip Area B. It is oval in shape, 3.3 cm. in length and 2.4 cm. in width. The edge is beveled flat; one surface is partially smoothed.

Nine pieces of miscellaneous ground stone were recorded from various proveniences. These range in length from 6.8 cm. to 32 cm. and in width from 6 cm. to 13 cm. All show evidence of grinding on one or more surfaces; three are whole, the remaining are either fragmentary or the condition cannot be determined.

Function in all cases cannot be determined accurately. One piece of ground and pecked stone was found in the floor fill of Kiva 1. It is cone shaped, 7.5 cm. in length and 7.6 cm. in width. The bit end is flattened and pecked slightly; the poll end flattened, with a circular depression in the center. The body of the stone is ground smooth and slightly pecked.

Ceramics

The total ceramic assemblage from Ariz. D:11:15 is only 2,225 sherds, all of which are Kayenta Anasazi types. Unlike the pottery from other excavated sites in 1968, the decorated types are dominated by Black Mesa Black-on-white suggesting Ariz. D:11:15 is slightly earlier. The occurence of Black Mesa Black-on-white is over twice as high as the next highest black-on-white type, Sosi Black-on-white. As usual, Tusayan Corrugated overwhelms in numbers the other types of Tusayan Gray Ware.

Four whole or partial vessels were recovered from the site. Two miniatures, one Tusayan White Ware bowl, and one Tsegi Orange Ware jar, were recovered from Burial 1. The white ware bowl is 4.8 cm. in height with a rim diameter of 11.4 cm. There is an interior design of two opposing sawtooth bands, and an almost circular black band on the bottom. There is no slip on the vessel. The orange ware has a Medicine Black-on-red design element in a checkerboard pattern. A handle is connected from the lip of the jar to the bottom of the neck. The

TABLE 14. *Provenience of pottery types from Ariz. D:11:15.*

Type	Surface	Strip A	Strip B	Strip C	Kiva 1	Kiva 1 Fill	Kiva 1 Fl. Fill	Test Tr'ches	Totals
Tusayan White Ware	1	7		2	7	29	1	121	168
Black Mesa B/W	2	14		6	11	22	4	45	104
Shato Variety								1	1
Sosi B/W		7		2	5	3	5	27	49
Dogoszhi B/W		2				9	2	15	28
Flagstaff B/W						3		2	5
Unclassified	2	5		2	1	17	5	57	89
Tusayan Gray Ware	1	12	3	2	6	13	8	101	146
Tusayan Corrugated	19	237	21	46	129	159	36	723	1370
Kiet Siel Gray								2	2
Moenkopi Corrugated		1		2	2	6		9	20
Tsegi Orange Ware	1	11	1		7	14	3	50	87
Medicine B/R		4				8		19	31
Tusayan B/R	1		1		6	18	2	31	59
Tusayan Polychrome						1		2	3
Tsegi R/O		1						1	2
Total	27	301	26	62	174	302	66	1206	2164

jar is 8.7 cm. in height and has a maximum diameter of 7.4 cm. A large fragmentary dipper with a Medicine Black-on-red design was recovered from the fill of Test Trench 4. The handle is missing, but the area of attachment can be discerned. The diameter is 11.5 cm., the height of the bowl is 5.3 cm. The remaining Tusayan White Ware vessel is fragmentary, only the rim and neck were intact. The neck was inserted and plastered into the kiva floor, possibly to serve as a storage area. The design consists of three rows of diamonds around the circumference of the neck; the bottom row of diamonds is hatched. The rim diameter of the neck is 12.6 cm.; the height, 8.2 cm.

Twenty whole or fragmentary *worked sherds* were recovered from assorted proveniences at the site. One Tsegi Orange Ware sherd was the only non-Tusayan White Ware worked sherd; it is fragmentary, with a length of 8.6 cm. and a width of 5.3 cm. Of the remaining nineteen sherds, seven are plain Tusayan White Ware. All are fragmentary and are basically sub-rectangular to oblong in shape. They range in length from 3.3 cm. to 9.2 cm., and in width from 4.1 cm. to 6.8 cm. Two fragmentary Tusayan White Ware sherds have a thick black line design present on the concave side. One is semi-circular, 6.2 cm. in length and 4.6 cm. in width. The other is oblong, 7.9 cm. in length, 4.4 cm. in width. Two Sosi Black-on-white worked sherds were recovered. Both are oval, with the design element on the interior of the sherd. Except for a small chip missing from the rim of one sherd, both edges are ground smooth. They are 12.7 cm. and 7.3 cm. in length, and 6.7 cm. and 6.9 cm. in width, respectively. A Dogoszhi Black-on-white design was found on three worked sherds. All are fragmentary, and each has one or more fragmented edges. They range in length from 4 cm. to 4.8 cm., and in width from 2 cm. to 6 cm. The remaining five sherds all have a Black Mesa Black-on-white design element. Of the five, three were located in the floor fill between the ventilator shaft and the deflector slab of the kiva. All are fragmentary and range in length from 3.9 cm. to 9.8 cm., and in width from 4.4 cm. to 6.8 cm. One or more of the edges have been ground on each sherd.

Human Burial

Burial 1

A single human burial was found in the approximate center of the trash zone (Appendix I). The child burial was placed in a prepared pit dug into sterile soil below the trash deposit. The pit is oval in outline, 47 cm. north-south and 40 cm. east-west. The maximum depth of the pit below the trash is 40 cm.

The burial consists of fragmentary skull, portions of the lower arms and several rib fragments. Although some erosion of bone has obviously taken place, it is apparent that only a portion of the individual was buried in this pit. Obviously the size of the pit could not have accommodated the individual. The two vessels placed with the burial were resting to the west of the skull which was also on the floor of the pit. It is doubtful that the skeletal material could have settled to that depth in the burial pit if the entire individual had been placed in the pit. The vessels placed with the burial are described in the ceramic section of the report. One vessel is a Medicine Black-on-red jar and the other is a Tusayan White Ware bowl.

Summary and Discussion

Ariz. D:11:15, excavated during November, 1968, is assigned to the late Pueblo II stage of the Kayenta Anasazi. Little information was gained on domiciliary structures of time period because of the indistinct pattern of the postholes and the robbing of stone by later peoples. Even an estimation of population at the settlement is difficult because of the lack of information on domiciliary structures.

Although few habitation structures could be identified, the amount of trash suggests that the site was occupied for more than one or two years. Without a good estimate of the population at Ariz. D:11:15, however, the determination of length of occupation is impossible.

Ariz. D:11:15 fits the pattern of other slightly later excavated sites. No trade material of any type, except chipped stone which could have been acquired on collecting expeditions, was found at the site. The people living in the settlement were provincial farmers existing mostly on cultivated products grown in the alluvial-filled basins surrounding the site and possibly along the Moenkopi Wash flood plain. There is little evidence of hunting activity.

Despite the fact that Ariz. D:11:15 is slightly earlier than the other excavated sites, little distinguishes it as earlier except the ceramic count. The differences may even be a result of partial destruction of the site by later nearby peoples. A distinguishing feature of Ariz. D:11:15 is the absence of a specialized mealing room and the absence of any mealing bins. The presence of two storage pits at the site is also unique, but I hesitate to suggest at this point that in the late Pueblo II period there was a greater emphasis on collected and gathered food.

Ariz. D:11:27

Introduction

Little can be said about Ariz. D:11:27 since most of the site has apparently eroded down Upper Moenkopi Wash. The late Pueblo I-early Pueblo II occupation is situated on a terrace at an elevation of 6,500 feet on a low bench approximately 250 m. north of Upper Moenkopi Wash.

The site lies within the confines of Peabody Coal Company J-27 Strip Area. The site is on a relatively severe slope of eroding brown sand. The numerous sandstone outcrops surround the few sherds and sandstone slabs on the surface. Virtually no grasses grow on the eroded surfaces and the few juniper trees in this vicinity have been eroded below their bases and into the root systems. The major water source for the site is the Upper Moenkopi Wash, the flood plain of which would have supplied ample agricultural land. Because of the extremely eroded condition of the site, six test trenches were excavated to determine if there was any depth to the cultural materials.

This site was indicated by a scattering of pot sherds and by large, thin partially shaped sandstone slabs, the type of which often are used in construction of the typical Pueblo I cists. There was no dark stain to the soil suggesting most of it had eroded away.

Since the test trenches yielded no artifacts and no evidence of humic stained soil, excavation was abandoned and little more can be said about this site.

TABLE 15. *Provenience of pottery types from Ariz. D:11:27.*

Type	Survey	Test Trenches 2 and 3	Total
Tusayan White Ware	6	4	10
Kana-a B/W	4	1	5
Black Mesa B/W	5		5
Unclassified		2	2
Lino Tradition	13	22	35
Kana-a Gray	5	20	25
Tusayan Corrugated	1		1
Total	34	49	83

CHAPTER FIVE

Conclusions

AT THE END OF THE FIRST SEASON'S WORK on Black Mesa, certain patterns are apparent while some of the questions posed in the introductory section of this report can be refocused. Still other questions, which were not considered before work began, take on great importance.

Forty-one Anasazi sites were recorded and six excavated. It is obvious that the number of surveyed sites is insufficient to reveal much demographic data. There is little doubt, however, that the prehistoric inhabitants of northeastern Black Mesa belong to the Kayenta Anasazi tradition and this was apparent before a shovel was put into the ground. The most obvious indicator of cultural affiliation is, of course, ceramics. A few sherds fit Colton's (1939) description of sherds diagnostic of the Tusayan Branch, but in the main, the ceramics are classic Tusayan White and Gray Wares of the Kayenta Branch.

There is more evidence that Black Mesa does not fit the typical Kayenta pattern architecturally. A tremendous degree of regional diversity in architecture is apparent throughout the Kayenta district. Kayenta architecture has been noted for its crudeness, but the architecture of Black Mesa surpasses even these bounds in poor quality. Recent excavations in the Kayenta region have underlined the fact that the pithouse was a common, if not favored, dwelling type through middle Pueblo III (Bliss 1960; Jennings 1966:56), yet no subsurface dwellings were encountered on Black Mesa. On the other hand, the jacal structure so common on Black Mesa is rare or absent in other parts of the Kayenta region. Anderson (1969) found no jacal structures 18–30 miles north of the Black Mesa excavations on the Shonto Plateau. Nevertheless, Anderson did not strip large areas to the old occupation surface at his so-called camp sites and jacal structures might well exist on the Shonto Plateau. Even masonry dwelling and kiva forms on the Shonto Plateau bear little resemblance to those on Black Mesa. The plaza orientation to sites occurs only rarely on Black Mesa. The doorway with the combination entry box, ventilator, and hearth common in the Glen Canyon area (Ambler et al. 1964: 98) is absent on the mesa. There is a suggestion from the Glen Canyon excavations that the entry box complex developed later than the occupation on Black Mesa. The disparity of Black Mesa architecture with other Kayenta forms may be due in part to the lack of excavated sites of this period in other Kayenta regions.

Kiva form is highly variable, always roughly circular rather than rectangular with or without a recess or bench, and with or without masonry lining. In all cases except one, the kiva was burned, suggesting a purposeful firing of the kiva during the abandonment of the settlement. The kiva at RBMV 551 was also burned. The ratio of dwelling units to kivas is extremely low on Black Mesa. Using the modern Pueblos as an analogy, it is difficult to see how these small sites could support a kiva society. We assume that the function of the kiva was different on Black Mesa from what it is in a modern Pueblo. Was the kiva society makeup different or was the kiva also used, in part, as a dwelling? In most cases, a large number of manos and metate fragments were found in the kivas. The questions cannot as yet be answered.

Burial patterns are difficult to determine because of the great disturbance in the burial grounds and the consequent disarticulation of the skeletons. In addition, the sample of individuals is small. A semi-flexed position was preferred and there was no discernible orientation to the body. In several cases, burial pits were excavated below the trash zone, and in one instance, the pit was covered with a large stone slab.

Artifacts are undistinguished, except for the usually well-constructed and decorated Kayenta pottery. The small number of overfired pieces producing a yellow or orange cast to the pottery introduces the tantalizing prospect that the people of Black Mesa were firing with coal.

Chipped stone, unobtainable on Black Mesa, is understandably rare, while there is found an abundance of ground stone artifacts. Ornaments are confined to a few ground siltstone pendants, finger rings, and an occasional shell bracelet fragment.

In spite of what would appear to be an excellent foraging environment, the evidence for hunting and gathering is rare. Few animal bones were found, despite the screening of large amounts of trash at the largest site, Ariz. D:11:3. However, the poor conditions for bone preservation may account for this as even floral remains are exceedingly skimpy. Hugh Cutler (personal communication), after examination of the profiles in the trash zone, said he had never seen a trash deposit of this time period with virtually no seeds or other evidence of floral material present.

Yet, the evidence of domesticated plant products is great because of the high number of manos and metate fragments, as well as the large number of specialized mealing rooms and mealing bins even in these small sites. Although not denying the possible importance of hunting and gathering, these people of Black Mesa can probably best be characterized as farmers. Not only were these people farmers, they were obviously provincial farmers. The sites are small and scattered with little evidence of trade goods or luxury items. There is no evidence for individual status differentiation and the evidence for intersettlement economic or religious cooperation is scanty. It appears that each settlement was an independent community consisting of a few extended families at the most, practicing subsistence agriculture with some reliance on hunting and gathering. That northeastern Black Mesa may have only seasonally been occupied cannot as yet be totally discounted.

That the Black Mesans were not totally isolated, backwater bumpkins, however, is demonstrated by the remarkable degree of similarity of the overall design styles and design style elements on the pottery of Black Mesa with that of other Kayenta areas. Enough interaction was occurring so that a different line of design evolution on pottery did not develop on Black Mesa. That this interaction was, however, primarily with other Kayenta peoples is suggested by the absolute lack of any sherds identified from the Anasazi traditions such as Mesa Verde or Chaco.

The apparent provincialness of the Black Mesa population and the trend in the population, *i.e.*, starting in the late A.D. 600's and terminating about A.D. 1200, may well be a result of this highland arid environment with a short growing season, although it is not yet possible to delve into the great debate of population fluctuations. The results of pollen analysis from excavated sites are so conflicting that a rational discussion of the prehistoric environment must await the results of the analysis of the 1969 pollen samples.

That northeastern Black Mesa was depopulated about A.D. 1200 is apparent and that the move was to the northern canyon lands of the Tsegi drainage system and perhaps to the southern extremities of Black Mesa, both lower and more moist regions, is demonstrable. Furthermore, it appears that the move was orderly and that all useful items were taken during the exodus. Few metates were found. All had been removed from their bins. The removal or destruction of metates at abandonment of a settlement is a strong Kayenta trait. Almost all manos are fragmentary or worn to uselessness. Few vessels or other artifacts were found on abandoned room floors.

It seems obvious that the prehistoric inhabitant of northeastern Black Mesa fits Jennings' (1966:63) description of the typical Anasazi. He is not the dweller of a large town nor an inhabitant of a "marginal" area. He is "backwoods" Anasazi specialized in "making agricultural miracles in an environment which today is regarded as unfavorable for cultivation of crops without irrigation."

Appendix I.

HUMAN SKELETAL MATERIAL FROM BLACK MESA, ARIZ.

Walter H. Birkby

Arizona State Museum

University of Arizona, Tucson

Ariz. D:11:3

THE HUMAN SKELETAL MATERIAL recovered by the Prescott College-Black Mesa Archaeological Project in the summer of 1968 was submitted for analysis to the Arizona State Museum Laboratory of Physical Anthropology by the project leader, Dr. George Gumerman.

The material, representing the remains of fourteen skeletons (one fetus, two infants, five children, four adult males, and two adults of indeterminate sex) was isolated in the laboratory into the least possible number of individuals present in a given burial. Therefore, whenever more than one skeleton was determined to be present, a postscript letter was assigned to the burial number.

Four of these isolated remains (2B, 4A, 4C, and 6C) consisted of only a single bone. It is not without possibility that some of these might be the scattered remnants of other designated burials (*e.g.,* 2B may be part of 3A; 4C may be part of 2C). However, since the materials were submitted as discrete burials, they were analyzed in just that manner.

The submitted material, for the most part, was in fair to poor condition with none of the skeletons complete enough, nor the adult sample size large enough, to warrant a metric and/or non-metric comparison with other skeletal populations.

Age and Sex: Distributions of age and sex for the separated individuals are given below in tabular form for quick reference. Their estimated ages (in years) are listed after each burial number. No female or adolescent material could be determined.

Fetus	Infant	Child	Male	Sex Indeterminate
B-1	B-3B (2-3)	B-2A (8-10)	B-3C (Adult)	B-2C (Adult)
	B-6C (2-3)	B-2B (4-6)	B-4B (18-23)	B-4C (Adult)
		B-3A (4-5)	B-6A (Adult)	
		B-4A (?)	B-6B (18-22)	
		B-5 (4-5)		

The ages of the pre-adult individuals were determined from Johnston's (1962) tables on long bone lengths of infants and children and also from states of dental development. The adult ages were determined from stages of epiphyseal union and from changes in the pubic symphysis (McKern and Stewart 1957) whenever these elements were available for study.

Stature: The morphological lengths of adult long bones were available for stature determinations in only three cases (4B, 6A, and 6B). Estimated living statures, employing Genoves' (1967) tables, were 5 feet 4 2/5 inches (163.5 cm.), 5 feet 3 1/5 inches (161.5 cm.), and 5 feet 1 4/5 inches (157.0 cm.) respectively for these adult males.

Deformation: Artificial cranial deformation of the lambdoidal variety was observed on two of the children's skulls (2A and 3A). The only other vault on which such an observation could have been made was the fragmentary skull of Burial 5, but this was in too poor a condition to evaluate properly. None of the adult inhumations contained sufficient cranial material on which observations for deformation could be made.

Pathology: Dental pathologies were observed on material from burials 3A, 4B, and 6A. The left maxillary deciduous first molar of 3A was carious. There was evidence of peridontal disease of the mandibular right alveolar border of 4B. The mandible of 6A bore evidence of abscessing of the right second molar which was missing antemortem. In addition there was antemortem tooth loss with complete alveolar resorption of the right first molar. The left second premolar, first molar, and second molar were also missing prior to death and had a complete resorption of the alveolar crest. The maxillary right central incisor of Burial 2A exhibited enamel hypoplasia. This condition, although not a pathology in itself, could nevertheless indicate that the individual had had one or more constitutional disturbances during the course of enamel formation of that tooth.

Osseous pathologies occurred in three of the burials. The 2A child had a possible advanced atrophic condition of the femurs (*i.e.*, a "knife-edge" medial border of the distal one-half with thinning of the cortex of the entire shaft) and resultant cortical demineralization of the bones of the lower legs. (I have noted this type of border-sharpening before in cases of anterior poliomyelitis, but with pronounced anterior curvature of the shaft. Such curvature was lacking in the case under consideration, and I suppose that nearly any neuropathy or myopathy might produce the "knife-edge" condition.) The cortical bone of the arms appeared essentially normal in thickness for a child of this age.

There was a small osteophyte (myostitis ossificans?) on the medial surface of the right proximal fibula of 6A. Another such osseous condition was noted on the anterio-superior surface of the medial epicondyle on the left humerus of 6B. If these manifestations are indeed myostitis ossificans traumatica, the former case may indicate injury and resulting ossification along the interosseous membrane of the fibula. The latter case (6B) might have resulted from injury to the left epicondylar region with ossification following along the medial intermuscular septum.

[121]

The Burials

B-1: The incomplete remains of a fetus. *Suggested* age is 4–5 lunar months (based on long bone measurements).

B-2A: Child, 8–10 years old. Represented by incomplete and fragmentary cranial and post-cranial remains. The left humerus, radius, and ulna are missing; both innominates and clavicles are missing as are all vertebrae and ribs, and the right scapula. There are rodent tooth marks on some of the long bones. Both femurs are atrophied with "knife-edge" disto-medial borders; the cortex of the bones of the lower legs is thinned while cortical thickness of the arm bones appears normal. Two loose teeth (a lower premolar and the upper right central incisor) are present. The latter is three-quarter double-shoveled with evidence of enamel hypoplasia.

B-2B: Child, 4–6 years old. This individual is represented only by a left tibia and a metatarsal.

B-2C: Adult, sex indeterminate. Represented post-cranially by fragmentary remains of the right radius and clavicle, a fragmentary left rib, and one phalanx.

B-3A: Child, 4–5 years old. Represented cranially by a well preserved skull with pronounced lambdoidal deformation. Elements missing from the post-cranial skeleton include both humeri, clavicles, and scapulae, the left tibia and radius, the right ulna, ilium, and fibula, and all but three vertebrae and two ribs. Dentally, only the four deciduous molars are *in situ*; the left maxillary deciduous first molar is carious.

B-3B: Infant, 2–3 years old. Represented post-cranially by a right ilium, pubis, and portions of the sacrum. One non-erupted permanent molar tooth bud is present.

B-3C: Male, adult (age indeterminate). Cranially, only portions of the right temporal and greater wing of the sphenoid are present. The post-cranial skeleton consists of a fragmentary left rib.

B-4A: Child, age indeterminate. This individual is represented by the seventh cervical vertebra only.

B-4B: Male, 18–23 years old. Cranially, only the mandible of this male is present. Post-cranially, all of the major long bones are represented although they are mostly fragmentary; however, morphological lengths could be taken on the right radius (239 mm.) and the left fibula (362 mm.). The estimated living stature, computed from these two bones, is 162.0 cm. and 163.5 cm. respectively. Four extant teeth are present in the mandible: the right and left first and third molars. Dental attrition is second degree (Hrdlicka 1952), and there is some indication of peridontal disease on the alveolus between the right canine and the first premolar.

B-4C: Adult, sex indeterminate. Represented by a first metacarpal only.

B-5: Child, 4–5 years old. Represented by a fragmentary skull, mandible, and post-cranial remains. The right scapula and left fibula are missing as are seven right and one left rib. Cranial deformation could not be determined from the fragments. All of the deciduous molars are erupted in the mandible and the right maxilla (the left is missing).

B-6A: Male, adult. Cranially, only the mandible is present with five extant teeth (right canine, first and second premolars; left canine and first premolar). Dental wear is third degree (Hrdlicka 1952). Post-cranially, both of the clavicles and innominates, the right tibia, ulna, and left fibula are missing. No vertebrae are present. The living stature of 161.5 cm. is based on an estimated morphological length (432 mm.) of the left femur. There is a small osteophytic growth occurring on the medial surface of the proximal right fibula. The mandibular right second molar is abscessed and missing antemortem; the left second premolar, first and second molar are missing antemortem; the four incisors are missing post-mortem.

B-6B: Male, 18–22 years old. No cranial material is present for this individual. Post-cranially, all of the leg bones as well as the vertebrae are missing. The estimated living stature of 157.0 cm. is based on the morphological length of the left radius (220 mm.). There is a cranially directed osteophyte on the anterio-superior surface of the medial epicondyle of the left humerus.

B-6C: Infant, 2–3 years old. The only bone present for this isolated individual is a non-fused lateral element of the neural arch from the first cervical vertebra.

Ariz. D:11:15

The osseous material submitted for analysis consisted of a fragmentary calvarium (cranium minus the face) and mandible, portions of both lower arms, debris of at least three ribs, and the remnants of two halves of the vertebral neural arch.

Very little metric or non-metric data could be derived from the cranial material as it was warped and in a poor state of preservation, although the left half of the mandible and the left parietal were seemingly better preserved. All of the deciduous dentition in the mandible had erupted prior to death and bore evidence of beginning attrition. The skull appeared to be lambdoidally deformed, but since there was some post-mortem warpage this observation must remain questionable.

One anomalous condition was observed in the mandible: the deciduous right lateral incisor was missing congenitally. No osseous pathologies were noted, but there was a carious deciduous left second mandibular molar.

Archaeologically, there was some question as to whether this was a disturbed primary burial. The question, unfortunately, cannot be resolved by an examination of the osseous remains. However, a macroscopic and microscopic examination of the bones does not reveal rodent tooth marks so often encountered in disturbed interments; nor are there any peculiar markings other than those produced by root action and/or soil nematodes.

REFERENCES

GENOVES, S.
  1967 Proportionality of the Long Bones and Their Relation to Stature Among Mesoamericans. *Amer. Journ. Phys. Anthrop.*, 26 1:67–77.

HRKLICKA, A.
  1952 *Practical Anthropometry*. 4th Ed. (T. D. Stewart, ed.). The Wister Institute of Anatomy and Biology, Philadelphia.

JOHNSTON, F. E.
  1962 Growth of the Long Bones of Infants and Young Children at Indian Knoll. *Amer. Journ. Phys. Anthrop.*, 20 3:249–253.

McKERN, T. and T. D. STEWART
  1957 Skeletal Age Changes in Young American Males. *Hdqts. O. M. Research and Development Command, Tech. Report EP-45*, Natick, Mass.

References

AMBLER, J. RICHARD, ALEXANDER J. LINDSAY, JR., and MARY ANNE STEIN
    1964   Survey and Excavations on Cummings Mesa, Arizona and Utah, 1960–1961. *Museum of Northern Arizona Bulletin 39, Glen Canyon Series,* No. 5, pp. 73, 98. Flagstaff.

ANDERSON, KEITH M.
    1969   Archaeology on the Shonto Plateau, Northeast Arizona. *Southwestern Monuments Association, Technical Series,* Vol. 7. Globe.

BAERREIS, DAVID A. and REED BRYSON
    1965   Climatic Episodes and the Dating of Mississippian Cultures. *The Wisconsin Archaeologist, New Series,* Vol. 46, No. 4. Milwaukee.

BANNISTER, BRYANT, JEFFREY S. DEAN, and WILLIAM J. ROBINSON
    1968   Tree-Ring Dates from Arizona C-D, Eastern Grand Canyon, Tsegi Canyon, Kayenta Area. *Laboratory of Tree-Ring Research, The University of Arizona.* Tucson.

BEALS, RALPH L., G. W. BRAINERD and WATSON SMITH
    1945   Archaeological Studies in Northeast Arizona. *University of California Publications in American Archaeology and Ethnology,* Vol. 44, No. 1. Berkeley.

BLISS, WESLEY L.
    1960   Impact of Pipeline Archaeology on Indian Prehistory. *Plateau,* Vol. 31, No. 1. Flagstaff.

BRETERNITZ, DAVID A.
    1966   An Appraisal of Tree-Ring Dated Pottery in the Southwest. *Anthropological Papers of the University of Arizona,* No. 10. Tucson.

BREW, JOHN OTIS
    1946   Archaeology of Alkali Ridge, Southeastern Utah: With a Review of the Prehistory of the Mesa Verde Division of the San Juan and Some Observations on Archaeological Systemics. *Papers of the Peabody Museum of American Archaeology and Ethnology, Harvard University,* Vol. 21, p. 302. Cambridge.

COLTON, HAROLD S.
    1939   Prehistoric Culture Units and Their Relationships in Northern Arizona. *Museum of Northern Arizona, Bulletin 17.* Flagstaff.

    1953   Potsherds: An Introduction to the Study of Prehistoric Southwestern Ceramics and Their Use in Historic Reconstruction. *The Northern Arizona Society of Science and Art,* pp. 65–66. Flagstaff.

    1955   Pottery Types of the Southwest: Wares 8A, 8B, 9A, 9B, Tusayan Gray, and White Ware, Little Colorado Gray, and White Ware. *Museum of Northern Arizona, Ceramic Series,* No. 3. Flagstaff.

1956　Pottery Types of the Southwest: Wares 5A, 5B, 6A, 6B, 7A, 7B, 7C, San Juan Red Ware, Tsegi Orange Ware, Homolovi Orange Ware, Winslow Orange Ware, Awatovi Yellow Ware, Jeddito Yellow Ware, Sichomovi Red Ware. *Museum of Northern Arizona, Ceramic Series,* No. 3C. Flagstaff.

COLTON, HAROLD S. and LYNDON L. HARGRAVE
1937　Handbook of Northern Pottery Wares. *Museum of Northern Arizona, Bulletin* 11. Flagstaff.

ELLIS, FLORENCE HAWLEY and LAURENS HAMMACK
1968　The Inner Sanctum of Feather Cave, A Mogollon Sun and Earth Shrine Linking Mexico and the Southwest. *American Antiquity,* Vol. 33, No. 1. Salt Lake City.

FOWLER, DON D. and C. MELVIN AIKENS
1963　1961 Excavations, Kaiparowits Plateau, Utah. *University of Utah Anthropological Papers,* No. 76. Salt Lake City.

GUMERMAN, GEORGE J.
1969　*The Archaeology of the Hopi Buttes District, Arizona.* Ph.D. dissertation, The University of Arizona, pp. 366–67. Tucson.

GUMERMAN, GEORGE J. and S. ALAN SKINNER
1968　A Synthesis of the Prehistory of the Central Little Colorado Valley, Arizona. *American Antiquity,* Vol. 33, No. 2. Salt Lake City.

HACK, JOHN T.
1942　The Changing Physical Environment of the Hopi Indians of Arizona. *Papers of the Peabody Museum of American Archaeology and Ethnology, Harvard University,* Vol. 35, No. 1. Cambridge.

HALL, EDWARD T., JR.
1942　Archaeological Survey of Walhalla Glades. *Museum of Northern Arizona, Bulletin* 20. Flagstaff.

HAYES, ALDEN C.
1964　An Archaeological Survey of Wetherill Mesa, Mesa Verde National Park, Colorado. *National Park Service, Archaeological Research Series,* No. 7-A. Washington.

HAURY, EMIL W.
1950　*The Stratigraphy and Archaeology of Ventana Cave.* The University of Arizona Press and the University of New Mexico Press. Tucson and Albuquerque.

JENNINGS, JESSE D.
1966　Glen Canyon: A Summary. *Anthropological Papers,* No. 81, *Glen Canyon Series,* No. 31, pp. 55–56. Salt Lake City.

LINDSAY, ALEXANDER, J., JR. and J. RICHARD AMBLER
1963　Recent Contributions and Research Problems in Kayenta Anasazi Prehistory. *Plateau,* Vol. 35, No. 3, p. 91. Flagstaff.

LINDSAY, ALEXANDER J., JR., J. RICHARD AMBLER, MARY ANNE STEIN and PHILIP
M. HOBLER
    1968   Survey and Excavations North and East of Navajo Mountain, Utah,
              1959–1962. *Museum of Northern Arizona Bulletin 45, Glen Canyon
              Series* No. 8. Flagstaff.

SCHOENWETTER, JAMES and ALFRED E. DITTERT, JR.
    1968   An Ecological Interpretation of Anasazi Settlement Patterns. *Anthro-
              pological Archeology in the Americas*, p. 52. Washington, D.C.

WHITE, ANTA M., LEWIS R. BINFORD and MARK L. PAPWORTH
    1963   Miscellaneous Studies in Typology and Classification. *Anthropological
              Papers*, Museum of Anthropology, The University of Michigan, No.
              19. Ann Arbor.

WOODBURY, RICHARD B.
    1954   Prehistoric Stone Implements of Northeastern Arizona. *Papers of the
              Peabody Museum of American Archaeology and Ethnology, Harvard
              University*, Vol. 34. Cambridge.